I0642225

Francis Aidan Gasquet

The Last Abbot of Glastonbury and His Companions

A Historical Sketch

Francis Aidan Gasquet

The Last Abbot of Glastonbury and His Companions
A Historical Sketch

ISBN/EAN: 9783337097745

Printed in Europe, USA, Canada, Australia, Japan

Cover: Foto ©ninafisch / pixelio.de

More available books at **www.hansebooks.com**

THE

LAST ABBOT OF GLASTONBURY

AND HIS

COMPANIONS

AN HISTORICAL SKETCH

BY

FRANCIS AIDAN GASQUET, D.D.

Of the Order of St. Benedict

London

SIMPKIN MARSHALL, HAMILTON, KENT & Co., Ltd.

—

1895

LONDON:
PRINTED BY
JOHN BALE AND SONS,
OXFORD HOUSE,
GREAT TITCHFIELD STREET, W.

DILECTIS · FRATRIBVS

MONACHIS · CONGREGATIONIS · ANGLICANAE

ORDINIS · SANCTI · BENEDICTI

ET · VOBIS · PRAESERTIM

CARIS · SODALIBVS

MONASTERII · SANCTI · GREGORII · MAGNI · DE · DOWNSIDE

A · PATRIBVS · PRO · FIDE · EXSVLANTIBVS

DVACI · OLIM · CONDITI

QVI · IN · PATRIAM · REDVCES

HAVD · LONGE · AB · VMBRA

VENERABILIS · GLASTONIENSIS · ECCLESIAE

FELICITER · SEDETIS

ATQVE · IN · TERRA · TOT · SANCTORVM · MEMORIIS · CONSECRATA

MOREM · VITAE · TENETIS

A · DIVO · PATRE · BENEDICTO · TRADITVM

DEDICATVR   HOC · OPVS · GRATISSIMI · CORDIS

IN · HONOREM · MARTYRVM

FLORVM · HVIVS · ANGLIAE · NOSTRAE

NECNON · EIVSDEM · REGVLAE

SVB · QVA · NOS · IPSI · MILITAMVS

INTER · QVOS · EMINET

VIR · VENERABILIS · ET · VLTIMVS · GLASTONIAE · ABBAS

RICHARDVS

IPSE · CVM · CONSORTIBVS · SVI · MARTYRII

PRO · NOBIS · AC · PRO · PATRIA · INTERCEDAT

CONTENTS.

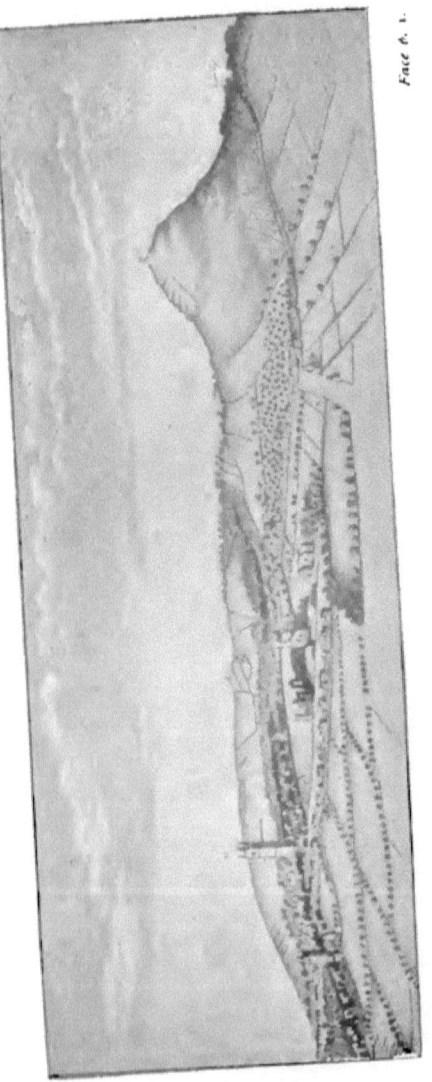

Face p. x.

VIEW OF GLASTONBURY AND THE TOR (from Hollar's print).

THE LAST ABBOT OF GLASTONBURY.

CHAPTER I.

GLASTONBURY.

THE prospect from the Roman camp of Masbury, on the Mendip hills of Somerset, is one to be remembered. The country presents itself to the view as in a map. In front a vast plain stretches out into the dim blue horizon across Dorsetshire to the shores of the English Channel. To the east the hills fall and rise like the swell of the sea in a series of vales and heights till they are lost in the distance. Westward the landscape is more varied, the ground, which at the spectator's feet had attained well-nigh to the dignity of a mountain, sinks away in a succession of terraces to the level country lying between it and the waters of the Severn sea. From the midst

of this plain there rises clear and sharp against
the sky, like a pyramid, a hill crowned with
a tower, which forms from all points the most
marked feature of the scene.   Neither the
glancing of the sunlight from the surface of
the sea some fifteen miles away, nor the
glimpse that is caught between the trees
of the grey towers and gables of the great
cathedral church of Wells, nor yet the sight of
the spire of Doulting, calling up as it does
memories of Saint Aldhelm, can long restrain
the eye from turning once again to gaze on the
conical hill with its tower which stands out in
the landscape.   Remarkable alike in its con-
tour and in its situation, these do not consti-
tute its chief attraction, for it speaks not only
to the eye but to the mind also ; it is Nature's
monument marking a spot of more than ordinary interest.   The shadows of tradition seem
still to hover over the hill and recall a past
which is lost in the dimness of legend.   More
than all, however, the last record which marks
the place in the pages of history brings to
mind a deed of desecration and of blood per-
petrated in the evil days which brought ruin

to the most famous sanctuary on English soil, for here suffered for conscience sake Richard Whiting, last abbot of the far-famed abbey of Glastonbury which nestled at its foot, thus making a worthy close to a history without parallel in the annals of our country.

The history of Glastonbury is the history of its abbey; without its abbey Glastonbury were nothing.[1] Even among those great ecclesiastical institutions, the Benedictine abbeys of mediæval England, the history of Glastonbury has a character all its own. I will not insult its venerable age, says a recent historian, by so much as contrasting it with the foundations of yesterday which arose under the influence of the Cistercian movement, for they play but a small part indeed in the history of this church and realm. Glastonbury is something more than Netley and Tintern, Rievaux and Fountains. It is something more again than the Benedictine houses which arose at the bidding of the Norman Conqueror, of his race and of his companions; more than Selby and Battle,

---

[1] The following is adapted from the late Professor Freeman.

and Shrewsbury and Reading.   It is in its own
special aspect something more even than the
royal minster of St. Peter, the crowning place
of Harold and of William, which came to sup-
plant Glastonbury as the burial place of kings.
Nay, it stands out distinct even among the
great and venerable foundations of English
birth which were already great and venerable
when this country fell into the hands of the
Norman.   There is something in Glastonbury
which one looks for in vain at Peterborough
and Crowland and Evesham, or even at Winchester and Canterbury; all these are the works
of our own, our English people ; they go back
to the days of our ancient kingship, they go
back—some of them—even to the days when
Augustine preached, and Theodore fixed the
organisation of the growing English Church ;
but they go back no further.   We know their
beginnings, we know their founders; their history, nay, their very legends do not dare to
trace up their foundations beyond the time
of the coming of Saxon and Angle into this
island.   At Glastonbury, and at Glastonbury
alone, we instinctively feel that the name of

England is not all, for here, and here alone,
we walk with easy steps, with no thought of
any impassable barrier, from the realm of Saxon
Ina back to that of Arthur, the hero king of
the British race. Alongside of the memory
and the tombs of the West-Saxon princes, who
broke the power of the Northmen, there still
abides the memory of the British prince who
checked for a generation the advance of the
Saxon.

But at Glastonbury even this is a small
matter. The legends of the spot go back to
the very days of the Apostles. Here, and here
alone on English soil, we are linked, not only
to the beginnings of English Christianity, but
to the beginnings of Christianity itself. We
are met at the outset by the tradition that the
spot was made sacred as the dwelling of a
multitude of the just, and its soil hallowed by
the bodies of numerous saints, "whose souls
now rejoice," says an ancient writer, "in the
possession of God in heaven." For here were
believed to have found a resting place the
twelve disciples of Philip the Apostle, sent by
him to Britain, under the leadership of Joseph

of Arimathea, who had buried our Lord. "We know not," continues our author in his simple style, "whether they really repose here,

EXTERIOR OF THE CHAPEL OF ST. MARY (COMMONLY CALLED ST. JOSEPH'S), COVERING THE SITE OF THE OLD BRITISH CHURCH, AND FORMING THE ATRIUM OF THE MONASTIC CHURCH.

although we have read that they sojourned in the place for nine years; but here dwelt assuredly many of their disciples, ever twelve in number, who in imitation of them led a hermit's

life until unto them came St. Patrick, the great
Apostle of the Irish and first abbot of the
hallowed spot. Here, too, rests St. Benen, the
disciple of St. Patrick ; here St. Gildas, the
historian of the British ; here St. David, bishop
of Menevia, and here the holy hermit Indractus
with his seven companions, all sprung from the
royal race. Here rest the relics of a band of
holy Irish pilgrims, who returning from a visit
to the shrines of Rome, turned aside to Glastonbury out of love to St. Patrick's memory and
were martyred in a village named Shapwick.
Hither, not long after, their remains were
brought by Ina, our glorious king."

Such stories of the mediæval scribe, however
little worthy of credit in point of detail, re-
present, there can be little doubt, a substantial
truth. For as in later centuries there were
brought hither even from far distant Northum-
bria the relics of Paulinus, and Aidan and
Ceolfrid, of Boisil, of Benet Biscop and of
others for security on the advance of the
Danes, so too in earlier dangers there were
carried to Glastonbury, to save them from the
blind fury of the pagan Saxon, all that was

most sacred and venerated in the churches of Christian Britain.

"No fiction, no dream could have dared," writes the historian, "to set down the names of so many worthies of the earlier races of the British Islands in the *Liber Vitæ* of Durham or of Peterborough. Now I do not ask you to believe these legends; I do ask you to believe that there was some special cause why legends of this kind should grow in such a shape, and in such abundance round Glastonbury alone of all the great monastic churches of Britain."

Though these Glastonbury legends need not be believed as the record of facts, still it has been well said that "the very existence of those legends is a very great fact." The simple truth is that the remoteness and isolation of Glastonbury preserved it from attack, until Christianity had won its way among the West Saxons. So that when at last the Teutonic conqueror came to Avalon, he had already bowed his head to the cross and been washed in the waters of Christian baptism. His coming was thus not to destroy, but to give renewed

life to the already ancient monastic sanctuary.
The sacred precincts, hitherto held by Britons
only, now received monks of English race some
time before King Ina, its new founder, following the example of his father, Cædwalla, after a
reign of seven and thirty years, resigned his
crown, to journey to Rome, desiring to end his
pilgrimage on earth in the near neighbourhood
of the holy places, so that he might the more
readily be received by the saints themselves
into the celestial kingdom.

And when later the Danes overwhelmed
the land, it was this hallowed spot that was
destined to be the centre from which not
merely a vigorous monastic revival spread
throughout England, but whence the kingdom itself was raised by a great reformer to
a new pitch of secular greatness ; for it was
here that Dunstan as a boy, brought by his
father on a pilgrimage to the churches of St.
Mary and St. Peter the Apostle, "built of olden
time," passed the night in prayer. Overcome
by sleep the boy saw in a dream an aged man,
clothed in snowy vesture, leading him, not
through the simple chapels and half - ruined

buildings which then occupied the site, but
through the fair alleys of a spacious church
and comely claustral buildings, whilst he told
him that thus was Glastonbury to be rebuilt by
him, and that he was to be its future head.
This, though but a dream, was yet a dream
which must have been related by Dunstan himself in after years.   The young day-dreams of
a strong nature have a tendency to realise
themselves in later life, and this boyish vision
of a renovated Glastonbury, the outward sign of
a new monastic spirit, manifests the workings
of a mind influenced, but prepared to be influenced, by the past memories and the present
decay of the holy place.   Nor did these early
images pass away in view of the brilliant pros-
pects that opened out before the young cleric,
who had all the advantages of personal capacity
and powerful connections, and so he betook
himself to remote and solitary Glastonbury, to
work out the realisation of his monastic ideals.
Dunstan built up its walls with the essentially
practical end of securing the primary require-
ments of monastic enclosure, and the buildings
were just like those he dreamed of in his boy-

INTERIOR VIEW OF THE CHAPEL OF ST. MARY, SHOWING THE RUINS
OF THE CHOIR THROUGH THE WEST DOOR OF THE ABBEY CHURCH.

hood. He threw on his brother Wulfric the
entire temporal business and management of
the estates, so that he, freed from the encum-
brance of all external affairs, might build up the
souls of those who had committed themselves

NORMAN DOORWAY OF ST. MARY'S CHAPEL.

to his direction. It was here at Glastonbury,
under the care of St. Dunstan, that St. Ethelwold was formed and fashioned to be the chief
instrument in carrying out his monastic policy.
Here, too, St. Elphege the martyr, and a suc-

cessor of Dunstan on the throne of Canterbury
lived his monastic life.   And from Avalon, too,
about the same time, went forth the monk Sig-
frid, as the evangelist of pagan Norway.

With such a history, such legends of the past
and such a renewal as the firm and lofty spirit
of Dunstan effected in its refoundation, it is
no wonder that the repute of Glastonbury
drew to it a crowd of fervent monks and
the ample benefactions of devout and faithful
friends, so that from henceforward there was
no monastic house in England which for splendour or wealth could compare with this ancient
sanctuary.   Through the later Middle Ages,
to the people of England Glastonbury was
a *Roma secunda.*   Strangers came from afar
to visit the holy ground, and pilgrim rests
marked the roads which led to it.   Foreigners
coming in ships which brought their freight
to the great port of Bristol, hardly ever failed
to turn aside to visit this home of the saints,
whilst memorials of the sanctuary were carried
by the Bristol merchants into foreign lands.

Even now, as it lies in ruin, the imagination
can conceive the wonder with which a stranger,

on reaching the summit of the hill, still known as the *Pilgrim's Way*, saw spread out before him Glastonbury Abbey in all its vast extent, with its towers and chapels, its broad courts and cloisters, crowned with the mighty church, the fitting shrine of the sacred relics and holy memories which had brought him thither.

CHAPTER II.

RICHARD WHITING.

NEVER, perhaps, was Glastonbury in greater glory than at the moment when Richard Whiting was elected to rule the house as abbot.

Richard Whiting was born probably in the early years of the second half of the fifteenth century. The civil war between the Houses of York and Lancaster was then at its height, and his boyhood must have been passed amid the popular excitement of the Wars of the Roses and the varied fortunes of King Edward IV. It is not unimportant to bear this in mind, since the personal experience in his youth of the troubles and dangers of civil strife can hardly have failed to impress their obvious lesson strongly upon his mind, and to influence him when the wilfulness of Henry brought the

country to the very verge of civil war, with its
attendant miseries and horrors.

The abbot's family was west-country in its
origin and was connected distantly with that
of Bishop Stapeldon, of Exeter, the generous
founder of Exeter College, Oxford. Its principal member was possessed of considerable
estates in Devon and Somerset, but Richard
Whiting came of a younger branch of the
family, numbered among the tenant holders of
Glastonbury possessions in the fertile valley of
Wrington. The name is found in the annals
of other religious houses. About the time of
Richard Whiting's birth, for example, another
Richard, probably an uncle, was *camerarius*, or
chamberlain, in the monastery of Bath,[1] an
office which in after years, at the time of his
election as abbot, the second Richard held in
the Abbey of Glastonbury. Many years later,
at the beginning of the troubles which involved the religious houses in the reign of
Henry VIII., a Jane Whiting, daughter of
John, probably a near relative of the Abbot

---

[1] Reg. Beckington f. 311.

of Glastonbury " was shorn and had taken the habit as a nun in the convent of Wilton;"[1] whilst later still, when new foundations of English religious life were being laid in foreign countries, two of Abbot Whiting's nieces became postulants for the veil in the English Franciscan house at Bruges.[2]

Nothing is known for certain about the childhood and youth of Richard Whiting; but it may be safely conjectured that he received his early education and training within the walls of his future monastic home. The antiquary Hearne says that " the monks of Glastonbury kept a free school, where poor men's sons were bred up as well as gentlemen's and were fitted for the universities."[3] And some curious legal proceedings, which involved an enquiry as to the Carthusian martyr, blessed Richard Bere, reveal the fact that as a boy he had been

[1] R. O. Chanc., *Inq. post mortem.*
[2] Oliver, *Collections illustrating the History of the Catholic Religion*, p. 135. This house returned to England on the French Revolution, and the high esteem with which it was regarded by English Catholics, persecuted at home or exiles abroad, still attends this venerable community, now established at Taunton.
[3] *History of Glastonbury*, preface.

"brought up at the charges of his uncle," Abbot Bere, in the Glastonbury school. The pleadings show that Richard Bere was probably the son of one of the tenants of the abbey lands, and among those who testify to the fact of his having been a boy in the school were " Nicholas Roe, of Glastonbury, gent," and " John Fox, of Glastonbury, yeoman," both of whom had been his fellow scholars " in the said abbey together,"[1] and Thomas Penny, formerly Abbot Bere's servant, who spoke to the nephew Richard as having been in the school at the monastery, whence as he remembered he afterwards proceeded to Oxford. What is thus known, almost by accident, about the early education of the martyred Carthusian, may with fair certainty be inferred in the case of Richard Whiting. The boy's training in the claustral school was succeeded by the discipline of the monastic novitiate : and it was doubtless in early youth, as was then the custom, that he joined the community of the great Benedictine monastery of the west country.

---

[1] *Downside Review*, vol. ix. (1890), p. 162.

2

Glastonbury, with its long, unbroken history, had had its days of prosperity and its days of trouble, its periods of laxity and days of recovery, and when Whiting first took the monastic habit report did not speak too well of the state of the establishment.   John Selwood, the abbot, had held the office since 1457, and under his rule, owing, probably in some measure at least, to the demoralising influence of the constant civil commotions, discipline grew slack and the good name of the abbey had suffered. But it would seem that, as is so often the case, rumour with its many tongues had exaggerated the disorders, since after a careful examination carried out under Bishop Stillington's orders by four ecclesiastics unconnected with the diocese, no stringent injunctions were apparently imposed, and Abbot Selwood continued to rule the house for another twenty years.

From Glastonbury Whiting was sent to Cambridge,[1] to complete his education, and his

---

[1] Probably to " Monks' College.' Speed, speaking of Magdalen College, Cambridge, says it " was first an hall inhabited by monks of divers monasteries, and therefore heretofore

name appears amongst those who took their
M.A. degree in 1483.[1] About the same time the
register of the university records the well-
known names of Richard Reynolds, the Bridget-
tine priest of Sion, of John Houghton and
William Exmew, both Carthusians, and all
three afterwards noble martyrs in the cause of
Catholic unity, for which Whiting was also later
called upon to sacrifice his life. The blessed
John Fisher also, although no longer a student,
still remained in close connection with the university, when Richard Whiting came up from
Glastonbury to Cambridge.

After taking his degree the young Benedictine monk returned to his monastery, and there
probably would have been occupied in teaching.
For this work his previous training and his

---

called Monks' College, sent hither from their abbies to the
universitie to studye. Edward Stafford, last Duke of Buckingham, &c., bestowed much cost in the repair of it, and in 1519
. . . . new built the hall, whereupon for a time it was called
Buckingham College; but the Duke being shortly after attainted,
the buildings were left imperfect, continuing a place for monks
to study in, until the general suppression of monasteries by
King Henry VIII."—Speed, *History of Great Britain,* 1632,
p. 1053.

[1] Cooper, *Athenæ Cantabrigienses,* p. 71.

stay at the university in preparation for his degree in Arts, would have specially qualified him, and in all probability he was thus engaged till his ordination to the priesthood, some fifteen years later.   During this period one or two events of importance to the monks of the abbey may be briefly noted.

In 1493, John Selwood, who had been abbot for thirty-six years, died.   The monks having obtained the King's leave to proceed with the election of a successor,[1] met for the purpose, and made their choice, without apparently having previously obtained the usual approval of the bishop of the diocese.   This neglect was caused possibly by their ignorance of the forms of procedure, as so long a time had intervened since the last election.   It may be also that in the long continued absence of the Bishop of Bath and Wells from his See they overlooked this form.   Be this as it may, Bishop Fox, then the occupant of the See, on hearing of the election of John Wasyn without his approval, applied to the king for permission to cancel the

---

[1] Pat. Rot. 8 Henry VII., p. 2, m. 11.

election. This having been granted, he success-
fully claimed the right to nominate to the office,
and on 20th January, 1494, by his commissary,
Dr. Richard Nicke, Canon of Wells, and afterwards Bishop of Norwich, he installed Richard
Bere in the abbatial chair of Glastonbury.[1]

In the fourth year of this abbot's rule, Somerset and the neighbourhood of Glastonbury was
disturbed by the passage of armed men—insurgents against the authority of King Henry
VII. and the royal troops sent against them—
which must have sadly broken in upon the quiet
of the monastic life. In the early summer of
1497 the Cornish rebels who had risen in resistance to the heavy taxation of Henry, passed
through Glastonbury and Wells on their way
to London. Their number was estimated at
from six to fifteen thousand, and the country
for miles around was at night lighted up by
their camp fires. Their poverty was dire, their
need most urgent, and although it is recorded
that no act of violence or pillage was perpe-

---

[1] Reg. Fox Bath et Wellen, f. 48. Pat. Rot., 9 Henry VII.
26.

trated by this undisciplined band, still their
support was a burden on the religious houses
and the people of the districts through which
they passed.

Hardly had this rising been suppressed than
Somerset was again involved in civil commotions. Early in the autumn of 1497 Perkin
Warbeck assembled his rabble forces—" howbeit, they were poor and naked "[1]—round
Taunton, and on the 21st September the ad-
vanced guard of the king's army arrived at
Glastonbury, and was sheltered in the monastery and its dependencies. The same night
the adventurer fled to sanctuary, leaving his
8,000 followers to their own devices ; and on
the 29th of this same month Henry himself
reached Bath and moved forward at once to
join his other forces at Wells and Glastonbury.
With him came Bishop Oliver King, who,
although he had held the See of Bath and
Wells for three years, had never yet visited his
cathedral city, and who now hurried on before
his royal master to be enthroned as bishop a

[1] B. Mus. Cott. MS. Vit. A. xvi., f. 166b.

few hours before he in that capacity took part
in the reception of the king. Henry had with
him some 30,000 men, when on St. Jerome's
day he entered Wells, and took up his lodgings
with Dr. Cunthorpe in the deanery.[1] The
following day, Sunday, October 1, was spent
at Wells, where the king attended in the Cathedral at a solemn *Te Deum* in thanksgiving for
his bloodless victory. Early on the Monday
he passed on to Glastonbury, and was lodged
by Abbot Bere within the precincts of the
monastery.

The abbey was then at the height of its
glory, for Bere was in every way fitted for the
position to which the choice of Fox had elevated
him. A witness in the trial spoken of above
describes Abbot Bere as " a grave, wise and
discreet man, just and upright in all his ways,
and for so accounted of almost all sorts of
people." Another deposes that he " was good,
honest, virtuous, wise and discreet, as well as
a grave man, and for those virtues esteemed in
as great reputation as few of his coat and calling

---

[1] *Historical MSS. Report,* i. p. 107.

in England at that time were better accounted
of."[1]   On the interior discipline and the exterior
administration of his house alike he bestowed a
watchful care, and under his prudent administration the monastic buildings and church
received many useful and costly additions.   At
great expense he built the suite of rooms afterwards known as "the King's lodgings," and
added more than one chapel to the time-
honoured sanctuary of Glastonbury.   At the
west end of the town he built the Church of
St. Benen, now commonly known as St.
Benedict's, which bears in every portion of the
structure his rebus.   His care for the poor was
manifested by the almshouses he established,
and the thought he bestowed on the prudent
ordering of the lowly spital of St. Margaret's,
Taunton.   Beyond this, Bere was a learned
man, as well as a careful administrator, and
even Erasmus submitted to his judgment.   In
a letter written a few years after this abbot's
death this great scholar records how he had
long known the reputation of the Abbot of

---

[1] *Downside Review*, ut sup., p. 160.

Glastonbury. His bosom friend, Richard Pace, the well-known ambassador of Wolsey in many difficult negotiations, had told him how to Bere's liberality he owed his education and his success in life to the abbot's judicious guidance. For this reason, Erasmus, who had made a translation of the sacred Scriptures from the Greek, which he thought showed a " more polished style " than St. Jerome's version, submitted his work to the judgment of the abbot. Bere opposed the publication, and Erasmus bowed to the abbot's opinion, which in after years he acknowledged as correct.[1] Henry the Seventh, who ever delighted in the company of learned men, must have been pleased with the entertainment he received at Glastonbury, where the whole cost was borne by the abbot.[2] It is possible, by reason of the knowledge the king then derived of the great abilities of Bere, that six years afterwards, in 1503, he made choice of him to carry the congratulations of

---

[1] Ep. lib. xviii., 46 ; Warner, *Glastonbury*, p. 213.

[2] The Wardrobe accounts show that while the king had to pay somewhat heavily for his stay at Wells, his entertainment at Glastonbury cost nothing.

England to Cardinal John Angelo de Medicis, when he ascended the pontifical throne as Pius IV.

CHAPEL IN THE NORTH TRANSEPT OF THE ABBEY CHURCH, SHOWING THE TOWER OF ST. JOHN'S CHURCH, GLASTONBURY.

The troubles of Somerset did not end with the retirement of the royal troops. Though the country did not rise in support of the Cornish movement, it appears to have some-

what sympathised with it, and at Wells Lord
Audley joined the insurgents as their leader.
For this sympathy Henry made them pay;
and the rebels' line of march can be traced by
the record of the heavy fines levied upon those
who had been supposed to have "aided and
comforted" them.   Sir Amyas Paulet—the
first Paulet of Hinton St. George—was one of
the commissioners sent to exact this pecuniary
punishment, and from his record it would
appear that nearly all in Somerset were fined.
The abbots of Ford and Cleeve, of Muchelney
and Athelney, with others, had extended their
charity to the starving insurgents, and Sir
Amyas made them pay somewhat smartly for
their pity.   Somehow Glastonbury appears to
have escaped the general penalty; probably
the abbot's entertainment of the king saved the
abbey, although some of the townsfolk did not
escape the fine.[1]   This severe treatment must
have had more than a passing effect.   The
generation living at the time of the suppression of the abbey could well remember the

[1] R.O. Chapter House, Misc. Box, 152, No. 24. See also
Somerset Archæological Society, 1879, p. 70.

event.   They knew well what was the meaning
of the heavy hand of a king, and had felt at
their own hearths what were the ravages of an
army.   This may go far to explain how it
happened that in Somersetshire there was no
Pilgrimage of Grace.

Meantime Richard Whiting had witnessed
these troubles, which came so near home, from
the seclusion of the monastic enclosure in which
he had been preparing for the reception of
sacred orders.   The Bishop of Bath and Wells,
Oliver King, had not remained in his diocese
after the public reception of Henry.   He was
much engaged in the secular affairs of the
kingdom, and his episcopal functions were
relegated to the care of a suffragan, Thomas
Cornish, titular Bishop of Tinos, also at this
time Vicar of St. Cuthbert's, Wells, and
Chancellor of the Diocese.   From the hands
of this prelate Dom Richard Whiting received
the minor order of acolyte in the month of
September, 1498.   In the two succeeding years
he was made sub-deacon and deacon, and on
the 6th March, 1501, he was elevated to the

sacred order of the priesthood.[1] The ordination was held in Wells by Bishop Cornish in
the chapel of the Blessed Virgin, by the

CHAPEL IN THE SOUTH TRANSEPT, GLASTONBURY ABBEY.

cathedral cloisters—a chapel long since de-
stroyed, and the foundations of which have
recently been discovered.

[1] Reg. O. King, Bath et Wellen Ep.

For the next five and twenty years we know
very little about Richard Whiting.   It is more
than probable that his life was passed entirely
in the seclusion of the cloister and in the exer-
cise of the duties imposed upon him by obedience.   In 1505, the register of the University
of Cambridge shows that he returned there,
and took his final degree as Doctor in The-
ology.   In his monastery he held the office of
"Camerarius," or Chamberlain, which would
give him the care of the dormitory, lavatory,
and wardrobe of the community, and place him
over the numerous officials and servants necessary to this office in so important and vast an
establishment as Glastonbury then was.

CHAPTER III.

RICHARD WHITING ELECTED ABBOT.

IN the month of February, 1525, Abbot
Bere died, after worthily presiding over the
monastery for more than thirty years. A few
days after his death, on the 11th of February,
the monks in sacred orders, forty-seven in
number, met in the chapter house to elect a
successor. They were presided over by their
Prior, Dom Henry Coliner, and on his proposi-
tion it was agreed that five days were to be
left for consideration and discussion, and the
final vote taken on the 16th. On that day,
after a solemn mass *de Spiritu Sancto* the
" great bell " of the monastery called the monks
into chapter. There the proceedings were
begun by the singing of the *Veni Creator* with
its versicle and prayer, and then Dom Robert
Clerk, the sacrist, read aloud the form of cita-

tion to all having a right to vote, followed by a
roll call of the names of the monks.   The book
of the Holy Gospels was then carried round,
and each in succession laid his hand on the
sacred page, kissed it, and swore to make
choice of him whom in conscience he thought
most worthy.   After this, one Mr. William
Benet, acting as the canonical adviser of the
community, read aloud the constitution of the
general council *Quia propter,* and carefully ex-
plained the various methods of election to the
brethren.   Then the religious with one mind
determined to proceed by the method called
" compromise " (*per formam compromissi*).
which placed the choice in the hands of some
individual of note, and unanimously named
Cardinal Wolsey to make choice of their abbot.

The following day the Prior wrote to the
Cardinal of York, begging him to accept the
charge.   Having obtained the royal permission
and after having allowed a fortnight to go by
for inquiry and consideration, he, on March
3rd[1] in his chapel at York Place, declared

---

[1] Hearne, *Adam de Domerham,* App. xcvii.

Richard Whiting the object of his choice.
The Cardinal's commission to acquaint the
brethren of his election was handed to a
deputation from the abbey consisting of Dom
John of Glastonbury, the cellarer, and Dom
John Benet, the sub-prior, and the document
spoke in the highest terms of Whiting. He
was described, for example, as "an upright and
religious monk, a provident and discreet man,
and a priest commendable for his life, virtues
and learning." He had shown himself, it
declared, "watchful and circumspect" in both
spirituals and temporals, and had proved that
he possessed ability and determination to
uphold the rights of his monastery.[1] This
instrument, drawn up by a notary and signed by
the Cardinal and three witnesses, one of whom
was the blessed Thomas More, was handed to
the two Glastonbury monks, who returned at
once to their abbey.

They arrived there on the 8th of March, and
met the brethren in the chapter house, where
they declared the result of the Cardinal's

---

[1] Hearne, *Adam de Domerham*, App. xcvii.

3

deliberations.   Then, at once, Dom John of
Taunton, the   precentor,   intoned   the   *Te
Deum*, and they wended their way, chanting
the hymn, from the chapter to the church, leading the newly elect.   Meantime the news had
spread   throughout   the   town.   The people
thronged into the church to hear the proclamation, and as the procession of monks with
Richard Whiting came from the cloisters we
can well picture the scene.   The nave of the
mighty church was occupied by " a vast multitude" eager to do honour to him who was henceforth to be their temporal and spiritual lord
and father.   The glorious sanctuary of Avalon,
enriched during ten centuries by the generous
gifts of pious benefactors, had received new
and costly adornments at the hands of the
abbot so lately gone to his reward.   The vault
ing of the nave, which then rang with the
voices of the monks as they sang the hymn of
praise, was one of his latest works.   The new-
made openings in the wall marked the places
where stood King Edgar's Chapel, and those
of Our Lady of Loretto, and the Sepulchre, more
fitting monuments than was the plain marble

RUINS OF THE CHOIR OF GLASTONBURY ABBEY CHURCH, SHOWING THE WEST
DOORWAY OF THE NAVE IN THE DISTANCE.

Face p. 35.

slab that marked his grave, of his love and
veneration for the ancient sanctuary of Glaston.
And as the monks grouped themselves within
the choir, the eye, looking through the screen
which ran athwart the great chancel arch—the
porta cæli—would have seen the glitter of the
antependium of solid silver gilt studded with
jewels, with which the same generous hand had
adorned the high altar.

Into this noble sanctuary the people of
Glaston crowded on that March morning in the
year 1525 to hear what selection the great
Cardinal had made.   And as the voices of the
monks died away with the last "Amen" to the
prayer of thanksgiving to God for mercies to
their House, a notary public, at the request
of the Prior and his brethren, turned to the
people, and from off the steps of the great altar
proclaimed in English the due election of
Brother Richard Whiting.   Then, as the
people streamed forth from the church bearing the news abroad, the monks returned to
chapter for the completion of the required
formalities.   And first, the free consent of the
elect himself had to be obtained, and he as yet

remained unwilling to take up the burden of so
high an office. He had betaken himself to the
guest-house, called the "hostrye," and thither
Dom William Walter and Dom John Winch-
combe repaired, as deputed by the rest, to win
him to consent. At first he determined to
refuse, and then demanded time for thought
and prayer ; but a few hours after, " being," as
he declared, "unwilling any longer to offer
resistance to what appeared the will of God,"
he yielded to their solicitations and accepted
the dignity and burden.

Then on Richard Whiting's acceptance being
notified to the Cardinal, he sent two commissioners to conduct the required canonical in-
vestigations into the fitness of the elect for the
office. On 25th March these officials arrived
at the monastery, and early on the morning following, the Prior and monks came in
procession to the conventual church ; in the
presence of the Prior and convent they made a
general summons to all and any to communi-
cate to them any facts or circumstances which
should debar Whiting from being confirmed as
abbot ; after this the like obligation was laid in

chapter on the monks.   Once more, at noon, the decree was published to a "great multitude" in the church, and afterwards fixed against the great doors.

Three days later, as no one had appeared to object to the election, the procurator of the Abbot, Dom John of Glastonbury, produced his witnesses as to age and character. Amongst them was Sir Amyas Paulet, of Hinton St. George, who declared that he had known the elect for eight-and-twenty years, which was just the time when Henry VII. had visited Glastonbury, and Sir Amyas had been occupied in extracting from the people of Somerset the fines levied for their real or supposed sympathy with Perkin Warbeck and his Cornish rebels.   The abbot's witnesses testified that he had always borne the highest character, not only in Somerset, but elsewhere beyond the limits of the diocese, and that none had ever heard anything but good of him. One who so testified was Dom Richard Beneall, who had been a monk at Glastonbury for nineteen years, and who declared that during all those years Richard Whiting had been reputed a man of exemplary piety.

When this lengthy and strict scrutiny was finished the Cardinal's commissioners declared the confirmation of the elect. Then, after the usual oath of obedience to the Bishop of the Diocese had been taken by the elect, he received the solemn blessing in his own great abbey church from Dr. William Gilbert, Abbot of Bruton and Bishop of Mayo in Ireland, at that time acting as suffragan to the Bishop of Bath and Wells.[1]

In the pages of ecclesiastical history Wolsey's name meets with scant favour. Writers of all parties, whether they look on him with friendly or unfriendly eye, have little to say of his devotion to the best interests of the Church. Whatever his defects, due credit has not been given him for the real and enlightened care which he bestowed on the true welfare of the religious orders. For the Benedictines and Augustinians he designed, and in part carried out, measures of renovation, the fruits of which were already visible when Henry suppressed the monastic houses. It is evident

[1] The account here given is from the official document in the Register of Bishop Clerke.

that he was not content with general measures,
but he fully acquainted himself with details and
with persons. The election of Abbot Whiting
is a case in point, and it is by no means improbable that the keen eye of the ecclesiastical
statesman had marked him out at the general
chapter of the Benedictines at Westminster,
over which the great Cardinal had himself
presided.

Thus was inaugurated the rule of the last
abbot of Glastonbury, amid the applause and
goodwill of all who knew him. Hitherto his
life had been passed, as the life of a monk should
be, in seclusion and unknown to the world at
large. He had clearly not been one to seek for
power or expect preferment, and his election to
the abbacy of Glastonbury, though causing his
name and fame to be spread wider, would after
all, in the ordinary course of events, have given
him in the main a local repute, and one of its
nature destined, after life's day well spent in
the peaceful government of his monastery, to
pass into oblivion. Of course his position as
head of one of the greatest of the Parliamentary abbeys (if the term may be used) obtained

for him a place, and that no undistinguished
one, in the roll of peers and in the House of
Lords; and thus he would be brought naturally
every year to the Court and the great delibera-
tive assembly of the realm.   But this was not
a sphere which attracted a man of Whiting's
temper and simple-minded religious spirit.
His place was more fittingly found within his
house, and in the neighbourhood which fell
within the direct range of his special and
highest duties.   Here, then, he might have
been best known and loved; and no further.
But another lot was marked out for him in the
designs of God.   His life was to end in the
winning of a favour greater than any which
could be bestowed by an earthly power, for
the crown of martyrdom was to be the reward
of his devotion to daily duty.   His fidelity to
his state and trust issued in a final act of
allegiance to Holy Church and to her earthly
head which causes his name to be known and
revered through all lands.

CHAPTER IV.

Troubles in Church and State.

The rule of Abbot Whiting over the vast establishment of Glastonbury had to be exercised in difficult times. Within a few months of his election Sir Thomas Boleyn was created Viscount Rochford, and this marked the first step in the king's illicit affection for the new peer's daughter, Anne, and the beginning of troubles in Church and State. For years of wavering counsels on the great matter of Henry's desired divorce from Katherine led in 1529 to the humiliation and fall of the hitherto all-powerful Cardinal of York.

Circumstances combined at this time to gather together in the social atmosphere elements fraught with grave danger to the Church in England. The long and deadly feud between the two " Roses" had swept away the pride and flower of the old families of England.

The stability which the traditions and prudent counsels of an ancient nobility give the ship of State, was gone when it was most needed to enable it to weather the storm of revolutionary ideas. Most of the new peers created in the fifteenth and sixteenth centuries to take the place of the old nobles had little sympathy, either by birth or inclination, with the traditions of the past. Many were mere place-hunters, political adventurers, ready if not eager to profit by any disturbance of the social order. Self-interest prompted them to range themselves in the restless ranks of the party of innovation. Those who have nothing to lose are proverbially on the side of disorder and change. The " official," too, the special creation of the Tudor monarchs, was by nature unsettled and discontented, ever on the look-out for some lucky chance of supplementing an inadequate pay. Success in life depended, for men of this kind, on their attracting to themselves the notice of their royal master, which prompted them to compete one with the other in fulfilling his wishes and satisfying his whims.[1]

---

[1] See Friedmann, *Anne Boleyn*, i., p. 27, seqq.

At the head of all was Henry VIII., a king
of unbridled desires, and one whose only code
of right and wrong was founded, at least in the
second half of his reign, on considerations of
power to accomplish what he wished. What
he could do was the measure of what he might
lawfully attempt. Sir Thomas More, after he
had himself retired from office, in his warning
to the rising Crumwell, rightly gauged the
king's character. "Mark, Crumwell," he said,
"you are now entered the service of a most
noble, wise and liberal prince ; if you will follow
my poor advice, you shall in your counsel
given to His Grace, ever tell him what he
ought to do, but not what he is *able* to do. For
if a lion but knew his own strength, hard were it
for any man to rule him."

Nor, unfortunately, were the clergy of the
time generally fitted to cope with the forces of
revolution, or hold back the rising tide of
novelties. In the days when might was right
and the force of arms the ruling power of the
world, the occupation of peace, to which the
clergy were bound, excited opposition from the
party who saw their opportunity in a distur-

bance of the existing order. The bishops
were, with some honourable exceptions, chosen
by royal favour rather than for a spiritual
qualification. However personally good they
may have been, they were not ideal pastors of
their flocks. Place-seeking, too, often kept
many of the lords spiritual at court, that they
might gain or maintain influence sufficient to
support their claims to further preferment.

The occupation of bishops over much in the
affairs of the nation, besides its evident effect
on the state of clerical discipline, had another
result. It created in the minds of the new
nobility a jealous opposition to ecclesiastics and
a readiness to humble the power of the Church
by passing measures in restraint of its ancient
liberties. The lay lords and hungry officials
not unnaturally looked upon this employment
of clerics in the intrigues of party politics and
in the wiles and crafty business of foreign
and domestic diplomacy as trenching upon
their domain and as thus keeping them out of
coveted preferment. Consequently, when occasion offered, no great difficulty was experienced
in inducing them to turn against the clergy

and thus enable Henry to carry out his policy of coercive legislation in their regard.

Five years after Abbot Whiting's election to rule over Glastonbury the fall of Cardinal Wolsey opened the way for the advancement of Thomas Crumwell, who may be regarded as the chief political contriver of the change of religion in England. On the fall of the old order he built up his own fortune. For ten years England groaned beneath his rule—in truth it was a reign of terror unparalleled in the history of the country. To power he mounted and in power he was maintained by showing himself subservient to every whim of a monarch, the strength of whose passions was only equalled by the remorselessness and tenacity with which he pursued his aims. Crumwell fully understood before entering on his new service what its conditions were, and neither will nor ability was lacking to their fulfilment. Under his management, at once skilful and unscrupulous, Henry mastered the Parliament and paralysed the action of Convocation, moulding them according to his royal will and pleasure.

Having determined that the great matter of his divorce from Katherine should be settled in his own favour, he conceived the expedient of throwing off the ecclesiastical authority of the pope over the nation and constituting himself supreme head of the Church of England. Though the clergy struggled for a time against the royal determination, in the end they gave way; and on November 3rd, 1534, the "Act of Supremacy" was hurried through Parliament, and a second statute made it treason to deny this new royal prerogative.

The sequel is well known. The clergy caught in the cunningly-contrived snare of premunire, and betrayed by Cranmer, who, as Archbishop of Canterbury, had inherited Warham's office, but not his spirit, were at the king's mercy. With his hands upon their throats Henry demanded, what in the quarrel with Rome was at the time a retaliation upon the pope for his refusal to accede to the royal wishes, the acknowledgment of the king as supreme head of the Church of England. Few among English churchmen were found

bold enough to resist this direct demand, or
who even, perhaps, recognised how they were
rejecting papal supremacy in matters spiritual.
As a rule, the required oath of royal supremacy
was apparently taken wherever it was tendered,
and the abbots and monks of Colchester, of
Glastonbury, and probably also of Reading,
were no exception, and on September 19th,
1534, Abbot Whiting and his community, fifty-
one in number, attached their names to the
required declaration.[1]

It is easy, after this lapse of time, and in the
light of subsequent events, to pass censure on
such compliance ; to wonder how throughout
England the blessed John Fisher and Thomas
More, and the Observants, almost alone, should
have been found from the beginning neither to
hesitate nor waver. It is easy to make light of
the shrinking of flesh and blood, easy to extol
the palm of martyrdom. But it is not difficult,
too, to see how reasons suggested themselves

---

[1] Deputy Keeper's *Report*, vii., p. 287. Mr. Devon, who drew
up the list, says: "The signatures, in my opinion, are not all
autographs, but frequently in the same handwriting ; and my
impression is, that the writer of the deed often added many
names."

at least for temporising. To most men at that
date the possibility of a final separation from
Rome must have seemed incredible. They
remembered Henry in his earlier years, when
he was never so immersed in business or in
pleasure that he did not hear three or even five
masses a day; they did not know him as
Wolsey or Crumwell, or as More or Fisher
knew him; the project seemed a momentary
aberration, under the influence of evil passion
or evil counsellors, and it was on the king's part
"but usurpation desiderated by flattery and
adulation;" these counsellors removed, all would
be well again. Henry had at bottom a zeal
for the faith and would return by-and-bye to
a better mind, a truer self, and would then
come to terms with the pope. The idea of the
headship was not absolutely new: it had in a
measure been conceded some years before,
without, so far as appears, exciting remon-
strance from Rome. Beyond this, to many
the oath of royal supremacy of the Church of
England was never understood as derogatory
to the see of Rome. While even those who
had taken this oath were in many instances

surprised that it should be construed into any such hostility.[1]

However strained this temper of mind may appear to us at this time, it undoubtedly existed. One example may be here cited. Among the State Papers in the Record Office for the year 1539 is a long harangue on the execution of the three Benedictine abbots, in which the writer refers to such a view :—

> I cannot think the contrary [he writes], but the old bishop of London [Stokesley], when he was on live, used the pretty medicine that his fellow, friar Forest, was wont to use, and to work with an inward man and an outward man; that is to say, to speak one thing with their mouth and then another thing with their heart. Surely a very pretty medicine for popish hearts. But it worked madly for some of their parts. Gentle Hugh Cook [the abbot of Reading] by his own confession used not the self-same medicine that friar Forest used, but another much like unto it, which was this: what time as the spiritualty were sworn to take the king's grace for the supreme head, immediately next under God of this Church of England, Hugh Cook receiving the same oath added prettily in his own

---

[1] Calendar, viii., Nos. 277, 387, &c., are instances of the temper of mind described above. No. 387 especially is very significant as showing the gloss men put on the supremacy oath, distinguishing tacitly between Church of England and Catholic Church, and "in temporalibus," and "in spiritualibus."

4

conscience these words following : "of the temporal church," saith he, "but not of the spiritual church." [1]

Nor from another point of view is this want of appreciation as to the true foundation of the papal primacy a subject for unmixed astonishment. During the last half-century the popes had reigned in a court of unexampled splendour, but a splendour essentially mundane. It was a dazzling sight, but all this outward show made it difficult to recognise the divinely ordered spiritual prerogatives which are the enduring heritage of the successors of St. Peter.

The words of Cardinal Manning on this point may be here quoted :—"It must not be forgotten that at this time the minds of men had been so distracted by the great western schism, by the frequent subtraction of obedience, by the doubtful election of popes, and the simultaneous existence of two or even three claimants to the holy see, that the supreme pontifical authority had become a matter of academical discussion *hinc inde*. Nothing but

---

[1] R. O. State Papers, Dom., 1539, No. 207, p. 23.

such preludes could have instigated even Ger-
son to write on the thesis *de auferabilitate
Papæ.* This throws much light on the singular
fact attested by Sir Thomas More in speaking
to the jury and the judge by whom he was
condemned, when the verdict of death was
brought in against him : ' I have, by the grace
of God, been always a Catholic, never out of
communion with the Roman Pontiff ; but I
have heard it said at times that the authority
of the Roman Pontiff was certainly lawful and
to be respected, but still an authority derived
from human law, and not standing upon a
divine prescription. Then, when I observed
that public affairs were so ordered that the
sources of the power of the Roman Pontiff
would necessarily be examined, I gave myself
up to a most diligent examination of that
question for the space of seven years, and
found that the authority of the Roman Pontiff,
which you rashly—I will not use stronger language—have set aside, is not only lawful, to
be respected, and necessary, but also grounded
on the divine law and prescription. That is

my opinion; that is the belief in which by the
grace of God, I shall die.'"[1]

The lofty terms expressive of papal prerogatives might pass unquestioned in the schools
and in common speech in the world, but from
this there is a wide step to the apprehension,
then none too common, of the living truths
they express, and a yet further step to that
intense personal realization which makes those
truths dearer to a man than life.

To some, in Whiting's day, that realization
came sooner, to some later. Some men, a few,
seized at once the point at issue and its full
import, and were ready with their answer without seeking or faltering. Others answered to
the call at the third, or even the eleventh hour;
the cause was the same, and so were the fate
and the reward, though to the late comer the
respite may perhaps have been only a prolonga-
tion of the agony.

It is of course impossible here to attempt
even a sketch of the train of events which led
to the destruction of Glastonbury and Abbot

---

[1] *Dublin Review*, January, 1888, p. 245.

Whiting's martyrdom. The suppression of the monasteries has been described as simply "an enormous scheme for filling the royal purse."[1] As his guilty passion for Anne Boleyn is the key to half of the extraordinary acts of the succeeding years of Henry's reign, so is the need of money to gratify his other appetites the key to the rest. From the seizure of the first of the lesser religious houses to the fall of Glastonbury, the greatest and most magnificent of them all, gain was the one thought of the king's heart. To this end every engine was devised, conscience was trodden under foot and blood was spilled.

With the evident design of obtaining a pretext for falling on the religious houses, the oath of supremacy in an amplified form was tendered to their inmates.[2] "There was presented to them," writes a recent historian, "a

---

[1] Dixon, *History of the Church of England*, i., p. 456. The last Abbot of Colchester, John Beche *alias* Marshal, is reported to Crumwell as saying : "The king and his council are drawn into such an inordinate covetousness that if all the water in the Thames were flowing gold and silver, it were not able to slake their covetousness." (R. O. State Papers, 1539, No. 207.)

[2] *Ibid.*, p. 213.

far more severe and explicit form of oath than
that which More and Fisher had refused, than
that which the Houses of Parliament and the
secular clergy had consented to take. They
were required to swear, not only that the chaste
and holy marriage between Henry and Anne
was just and legitimate, and the succession
good in their offspring," but "also that they
would ever hold the king to be head of the
Church of England, that the Bishop of Rome,
who in his bulls usurped the name of Pope and
arrogated to himself the primacy of the most
High Pontiff, had no more authority and jurisdiction than other bishops of England or elsewhere in their dioceses, and that they would
for ever renounce the laws, decrees and canons
of the Bishop of Rome, if any of them should
be found contrary to the law of God and Holy
Scripture."[1]   This scheme failed, "for the oath
was taken in almost every chapter-house where
it was tendered."

---

[1] *Ibid.*, p. 211.

CHAPTER V.

RICHARD WHITING AS ABBOT OF GLASTONBURY.

THE first years of Abbot Whiting's rule passed smoothly so far as the acts of his administration and his life at Glastonbury were concerned. He had of course to meet the troubles and trials incidental to a position such as was his. Moreover, for one who by his high office was called on to take a part, in some measure at least, in the great world of politics and public life, it could not be but that his soul must have been disturbed by anticipations of difficulties, even of dangers, in the not very distant future. Still, his own home was so far removed from the turmoils of the court and the ominous rumblings of the coming storm that he was able to rule it in peace. Discipline well maintained, a prudent and successful administration

of temporals and kindly relations with his neighbours, high and low, were certain evidences that
the government of Abbot Richard Whiting was
happy and prosperous. Under such circumstances the position which he occupied as a
peer of Parliament and as master of great
estates was one which, as the world might
say, even from its point of view, was eminently
enviable.

It is somewhat difficult in these days to form
a just and adequate idea of the place held in
the country by one who filled the abbatial chair
of Glastonbury. For wealth and consideration, though not indeed for precedence, it may
not unjustly be described as the most desirable
ecclesiastical preferment in England. The
revenues of the abbey exceeded those of the
archbishopric of Canterbury itself, whilst,
although the abbot had to maintain a large
community and a great household, still he was
exempt from the vast burdens necessarily entailed on so lofty a position as that of Primate
of England, who was *Legatus natus* of the Holy
See and often a Cardinal. The annual value of
the endowments of Westminster was, it is true,

THE PEGGED GRACE CUP OF GLASTONBURY ABBEY, NOW IN THE
POSSESSION OF LORD ARUNDELL OF WARDOUR.

Face p. 57.

slightly greater, but the ecclesiastical position of
an abbot of that royal monastery was singularly
diminished by the presence in his near neighbourhood of two such great churchmen as the
Archbishop of Canterbury and the Bishop of
London, whilst in its worldly aspect Westminster was overshadowed by the splendour of
the regal court at its doors. Glastonbury in
the sixteenth century had no rival in its own
district; the day was past when the aspiring
Church of Wells could raise pretensions on that
score. In the west country there was neither
prince nor prelate, certainly since the fall of the
Duke of Buckingham, to compare in position,
all considered, with the Abbot of Glastonbury.

But withal there existed in the court of the
abbot, for his household was regulated like that
of a court, a simplicity befitting the monastic
profession. His own house was large, its rooms
were stately, but it did not pretend to the
dimensions of a palace. He had a body of
gentry to wait upon him and grace the hospitality he was ready to show to visitors the
most distinguished and to the poorer classes
who thronged the monastic guest-hall. To

the great gate of the abbey, every Wednesday
and Friday, the poor flocked for relief in their
necessities, and as many as five hundred

RUINS OF THE ABBOT'S GUEST-KITCHEN, ERECTED IN THE
EARLY PART OF THE 14TH CENTURY.

persons are said to have been entertained at
times at the abbot's table. Still, a combined
simplicity and stateliness characterised the
whole rule of Abbot Whiting, and it is no

wonder that, as we are told, during his abbacy
some three or four hundred youths of gentle
birth received their first training in the abbot's
quarters.

It may be asked by some how in such a
position as this, surrounded by all the world
most ambitions, Abbot Whiting could still be
a monk. The position was not of his making ;
he found it. But that he should ever remain
a monk, that, as abbot, he should be a true
guardian of the souls committed to him, the
true father and pattern of his spiritual children,
that was by God's grace still in his power.
That he was all this, his very enemies have
testified, and the explanation is simple. Raised
to rule and command at an age when, as he
knew, the grave could not be far distant, he
was already a monk trained, disciplined, per-
fected in outward habit and in the possession
of his soul by his long course of obedience.
Tradition, which is often so true in matters of
small moment, more than a century and a half
after his death, still pointed out among the
ruins of his house, in the abbot's simple
chamber, Abbot Whiting's bed. It was

"without tester or post, was boarded at bottom, and had a board nailed shelving at the head."

A GLASTONBURY CHAIR, DATING FROM THE TIME OF ABBOT WHITING, PROBABLY MADE BY HIS FELLOW MARTYR JOHN THORNE (from the Engraving in Warner).

This bedstead, according to the tradition of the place, was the same that Abbot Whiting lay on, and "I was desired," writes the visitor who describes it, "to observe it as a curiosity." The existence of the tradition is proof

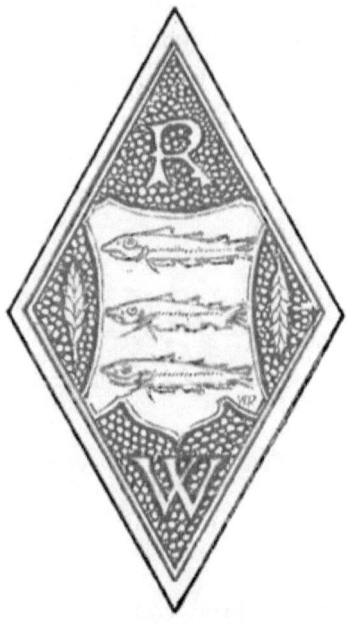

ABBOT WHITING'S STAMP ON THE BINDING OF HIS REGISTER NOW ADDITIONAL. MS. 17,451 (somewhat enlarged).

at least of an abiding belief, on the spot, in the simplicity of life of the last lord of that glorious pile, the vast ruins of which were

evidence of the greatness of the monastery.
It was possible even for an Abbot of
Glastonbury to preserve the true spirit of
poverty, and this was the secret of that excellent discipline which Dr. Layton to his
bitter disappointment found to exist at Glastonbury. The abbot practised first what, as his
duty imposed, he required from those entrusted
to his care, that is, from his spiritual children,
the monks of his house.

ANOTHER STAMP ON THE SAME BINDING (also enlarged).

It was during these comparatively peaceful
and happy times that Leland, the antiquary, on
his journey through England in search of an-
tiquities, and especially manuscripts, visited the
abbey. He was introduced to the iibrary by
Abbot Whiting in person, "a man truly upright

and of spotless life and my sincere friend " as
he calls him.[1] He was filled with amazement
at the treasures contained in the Glastonbury
library. " No sooner did I pass the threshold,"
he writes, "than I was struck with awe and
astonishment at the mere sight of so many remains of antiquity." He considered that the
library had scarce any equal in all England, and
spent some days in examining the shelves and
the many wonderful manuscripts he found
there.

With the conclusion of Henry's divorce case
came the end of these peaceful years of Abbot
Whiting's rule. Now began the anxious days
which were to end for him in the death of the
traitor, so far at least as the king's power could
extend in death.

Within a year from the general oath-taking
throughout England, and its failure to bring

---

[1] Hearne, *History of Glastonbury*, p. 67. ; *cf.* Walcott's *English Minsters,* ii., 129. Leland spoke of Abbot Whiting as "homo
sane candidissimus et amicus meus singularis," and " though,"
says Warner (*History of Glastonbury*, p. 219) " the too cautious
antiquary in after times passed his pen through this language
of praise and kindness, lest it should be offensive to his contem-
poraries, yet happily for the abbot's fame the tribute is still
legible and will remain for ages a sufficient evidence of the
sacrifice of a guileless victim to the tyranny of a second Ahab."

about the hoped-for result, Crumwell, ever
fertile in expedients, had organised a general
visitation of religious houses.   The instruments
he made choice of to conduct this scrutiny, and
the methods they employed, leave no doubt
that the real object was the destruction of the
monasteries under the cloak of reformation.
The injunctions are minute and exacting ; in
detail many were excellent ; as a whole, even
in the hands of persons sincerely desirous of
maintaining discipline and observance, they
were unworkable.   In the hands of Crumwell's
agents they were, as they were designed to be,
intolerable.   It was rightly calculated that
under the pretence of restoring discipline they
strike at the authority of religious superiors by
the encouragement given to a system of tale-
bearing.   By other provisions the monasteries
were, with show of zeal for religion, turned into
prisons and reduced, if it were possible, to such
abodes of misery and unhappiness as the unin-
formed Protestant imagination pictures them to
be.[1]   The moral of this treatment is summed

---

[1] *Henry VIII. and the English Monasteries*, i., chapter vii.,
"The Visitation of the Monasteries in 1535-6."   Dixon, vol. i.,
p. 357.

up by John ap-Rice and Thomas Legh, two of
the royal visitors, in a letter to Crumwell :

> By this ye may see [they write] that they [the re-
> ligious] shall not need to be put forth, but that they will
> make instant suit themselves, so that their doing shall
> be imputed to themselves and no other. Although I
> reckon it well done that all were out, yet I think it were
> best that at their own suits they might be dismissed to
> avoid calumniation and envy,[1] *and so compelling them to
> observe these injunctions ye shall have them all to do shortly*,
> and the people shall know it the better that it cometh
> upon their suit, if they be not discharged straight while
> we be here, for then the people would say that we went
> for nothing else, even though the truth were contrary.[2]

Armed with a commission to visit and
enforce the injunctions, Dr. Richard Layton,
the most foul-mouthed and foul-minded ribald
of them all, as his own letters testify, came to
Glastonbury on Saturday, August 21st, 1535.
From St. Augustine's, Bristol, whither he departed on the following Monday, he wrote to
Crumwell a letter showing that even he, chief
among a crew who "could ask unmoved such
questions as no other human being could have

---

[1] He means *invidia*, *i.e.*, public odium.
[2] Gairdner, *Calendar of Papers Foreign and Domestic*, ix.
No. 708. See also *Henry VIII. and the English Monasteries*,
i., p. 257.

imagined or known how to put, who could
extract guilt from a stammer, a tremble or a
blush, or even from indignant silence as surely
as from open confession "[1]—even Layton retired baffled from Glastonbury under the
venerable Abbot Whiting's rule, though he
covered his defeat with impudence unabashed.
"At Bruton and Glastonbury," he explains,
"there is nothing notable ; the brethren be so
straight kept that they cannot offend : but fain
they would if they might, as they confess, and
so the fault is not with them."[2]

At this period it would seem that Richard
Layton also spoke to the king in praise of
Abbot Whiting. For this error of judgment,
when some time later Crumwell had assured
himself of the abbot's temper, he was forced to

---

[1] Dixon, i., p. 357.

[2] Wright, *The Suppression of the Monasteries*, p. 59. Godwin,
the Protestant Bishop of Hereford, says that the monks, "following the example of the ancient fathers, lived apart from the
world religiously and in peace, eschewing worldly employments,
and wholly given to study and contemplation ;" and the editor
of Sander, writing when the memory of the life led at Glastonbury was still fresh in men's minds, says that the religious were
noted for their maintenance of common life, choral observance
and enclosure.

sue for pardon from both king and minister.
" I must therefore," he writes, "now in this my
necessity most humbly beseech your lordship
to pardon me for that my folly then committed,
as ye have done many times before, and of
your goodness to instigate the king's highness
majesty, in the premises."[1]

Hardly had the royal inquisitor departed
than it was found at Glastonbury, as elsewhere,
that the injunctions were not merely im-
practicable, but subversive of the first principles of religious discipline. Abbot Whiting,
like so many religious superiors at this time,
petitioned for some mitigation. Nicholas Fitz-
James,[2] a neighbour, dispatched an earnest
letter to Crumwell in support of the abbot's
petition.

" I have spoken," he writes, " with my Lord
Abbot of Glastonbury concerning such injunctions as were given him and his convent by
your deputy at the last visitation there. . .

---

[1] R. O. *Crumwell Correspondence*, vol. xx., No. 14.

[2] Probably a relative of Chief Justice FitzJames, and
grandfather of the first monk afterwards professed in the
English Benedictine monastery of St. Gregory's, Douai.

To inform your mastership of the truth there
be certain officers—brothers of the house—
who have always been attendant on the abbot,
as his chaplain, steward, cellarer, and one or
two officers more, (who) if they should be
bound to the first two articles, it should much
disappoint the order of the house, which hath
long been full honourable.   Wherefore, if it
may please your said good mastership to
license the abbot to dispense with the two first
articles, in my mind you will do a very good
deed, and I dare be surety he will dispense
with none but with such as shall be necessary.
.   .   .   Other articles there are which they
think very straight, howbeit they will sue to
your good mastership for that at more leisure ;
and in the meantime I doubt not they will
keep as good religion as any house of that
order within this realm."[1]

A month after this letter of Nicholas Fitz-
James, Abbot Whiting himself ventured to
present a grievance of another kind, affecting
others than his community.   The recent sus-
pension by royal authority of the jurisdiction

---

[1] Wright, *Suppression of the Monasteries*, p. 64.

exercised by the abbey over the town of Glastonbury and its dependencies, had caused the gravest inconveniences. There are many "poor people," he writes. "who are waiting to have their causes tried," and he adds that he cannot believe that the king's pleasure has been rightly stated in Doctor Layton's orders.[1] What the result of this application may have been does not appear, but it was clearly the royal purpose to let inconveniences be felt, not to remove them.

The proceedings taken in 1536 in regard to the suppression of the lesser monasteries must have filled the minds of men of Whiting's stamp with deep anxiety, as revealing more and more clearly the settled purpose of the king. "All the wealth of the world would not be enough to satisfy and content his ambition," writes Marillac, the French ambassador, to his master, Francis I. To enrich himself he would not hesitate to ruin all his subjects.[2] The State papers of the period bear ample witness to the

---

[1] R.O. *Crumwell Corr.* xiii. f. 58.

[2] *Inventaire analytique. Correspondance politique de M.M. Castillion et Marillac,* 1537-1542. Ed. J. Kaulek. No. 242.

justice of this sweeping statement.[1] The monasteries which were yet allowed to stand were
drained of their resources by ever-increasing
demands on the part of Henry and his creatures.   Farm after farm, manor after manor
was yielded up in compliance with requests
that were in reality demands.   Pensions in
ever-increasing numbers were charged on monastic lands at the asking of those whom it was
impossible to refuse.

Abbot Whiting was allowed no immunity
from this species of tyrannical oppression.
The abbey, for instance, had of their own free
will granted to blessed Sir Thomas More a
corrody or annuity.   On his disgrace Crumwell
urged the king's "pleasure and commandment"
that this annuity should be transferred to himself under the convent seal.   For a friend
Crumwell asks (and for the king's vicegerent
to ask was to receive) "the advocation of our
parish church of Monketon, albeit that it was
the first time that ever such a grant was made."
A further request, for the living of Batcombe,

---

[1] The volumes of Crumwell's correspondence in the Record
Office contain abundant evidence.

Whiting was unable to comply with, since
another of the king's creatures had been before-
hand and secured the prize. In one instance
an office which Crumwell had already asked
for and obtained from the abbot, he a few
months after demands for his friend " Mr.
Maurice Berkeley ; " and because the place was
already gone, he requests that the abbot will
in lieu thereof give the rents of " his farm

at Northwood Park." Abbot Whiting took
an accurate view of the situation : " If you
request it, I must grant it," he says ; and
adds, " I trust your servant will be content
with the park itself, and ask no more."

The extant letters of Abbot Whiting, for
the most part answers to such like applications
for offices or benefices in his gift, are marked
by a courteous consideration and a readiness to

comply up to the utmost limits of the possible. It is, moreover, evident that he had an intimate concern in all the details of the complex administration of a monastery of such extent and importance with its thousand interests, no 'less than a determining personal influence on the religious character of his community ; and that public calls were never allowed to come between him and the primary and immediate duties of the abbot.   He is most at home in his own country, among his Somersetshire neighbours, and in the "straight" charge of his spiritual children.   Confident too in the affection with which he was regarded by the population, he had no scruples, whatever may have been his mind in subscribing to the Supremacy declaration of 1534, in securing for his monks and his townsfolk in his own abbey church the preaching of a doctrine by no means in accord with the royal theories and wishes on the subject.   Thus on a Sunday in the middle of February, 1536, a friar called John Brynstan, preaching in the abbatial church at Glastonbury to the people of the neighbourhood, said " he would be one of them

that should convert the new fangles and new
men, otherwise he would die in the quarrel."[1]

By chance a glimpse is afforded of the
popular feeling in the district by a letter ad-
dressed to Crumwell by one of his agents,
always ready to spy upon their neighbours and
report them to their master, in the hopes of
gaining thereby the good graces of the all-
powerful minister.   Thomas Clarke writes
that one John Tutton of Mere, next Glaston,
—now by the way safely lodged in gaol—had
used seditious words against the king and had
spoken great slander against Crumwell himself.
The depositions forwarded with this letter
explain how Tutton had called one Poole a
heretic for working on St. Mark's day.   Poole
had replied that so the king had ordered, and
upon this Tutton declared that they could not
be bound to keep the king's command "if it
was nought, as this was," and he added that
" Lord Crumwell was a stark heretic."   Nor did
he stop here, for he continued in this strain ;
" Marry, many things be done by the king's

---

[1] *Calendar*, x., 318.

Council which I reckon he knoweth little of,
but that by such means he hath gathered great
treasure together I wot well; there is a sort
that ruleth the king of whom I trust to see a

ABBOT WHITING'S WATCH AND PRIVATE SEAL, NOW IN THE MUSEUM AT
GLASTONBURY (from the engraving in Warner).

day when they shall have less authority than
they have."[1]

Knowing doubtless what would be the nature

---

[1] Gairdner, *Calendar*, xi., No. 567.

of its business, Abbot Whiting, excusing himself
on the plea of age and ill-health, did not attend
the parliament of 1539, which, so far as it could
do, sealed the fate of the monasteries as yet
unsuppressed. He awaited the end on his own
ground and in the midst of his own people.
He was still as solicitous about the smallest
details of his care as if the glorious abbey were
to last *in ævum.* Thus an interesting account
of Abbot Whiting at Glastonbury is given in an
official examination regarding some debt, held
a few years after the abbot's martyrdom. John
Watts, "late monk and chaplain to the abbot,"
said that John Lyte, the supposed debtor, had
paid the money "in manner and form following.
That is to say, he paid £10 of the said £40 to
the said abbot in the little parlour upon the
right hand within the great hall, the Friday
after New Year's Day before the said abbot
was attainted. The said payment was made
in gold" in presence of the witness and only
one other : "for it was immediately after the
said abbot had dined, so that the abbot's gentlemen and other servants were in the hall at
dinner." Also "upon St. Peter's day at mid-

summer, being a Sunday, in the garden of the said abbot at Glastonbury, whilst high mass was singing," the debtor "made payment" of the rest. "And at that time the abbot asked of the said master Lyte whether he would set up the said abbot's arms in his new buildings that he had made. And the said master Lyte answered the said abbot that he would ; and so at that time the said abbot gave unto the said Mr. Lyte eight angels nobles.   And at the payment of the £30 there was in the garden at that time the Lord Stourton.   I suppose," continues the witness, "that the said Lord Stourton saw not the payment made to the abbot, for the abbot got him into an arbour of bay in the said garden and there received his money.   And very glad he was at that time that it was paid in gold for the short telling, as also he would not, by his will, have it seen at that time."[1] Thus too almost the last glimpse afforded of the

[1] R. O. Exch. Augt. Off. Misc. Bk., xxii., Nos. 13-18.   In view of the circumstances of the time it seems likely that the witness was anxious to ward off any possibility of Lord Stourton being mixed up in the affair.   This anxiety to save friends from embarrassing examinations is a very common feature in documents of this date.

last Abbot of Glastonbury in his time-honoured home shows him in friendly converse with his near neighbour, Lord Stourton, who was the head of an ancient race which popular tradition had justly linked for centuries with the Benedictine order, and which even in the darkest days of modern English Catholicity proved itself a firm and hereditary friend.

Before passing on to the closing acts of the venerable abbot's life and to his martyrdom, it is necessary to premise a few words on suppression in its legal aspect. There seems to be abroad an impression that the monasteries were all, in fact, dissolved by order of Parliament, and accordingly that a refusal of surrender to the king, such as is found at Glastonbury, was an act which, however morally justifiable as a refusal to betray a trust, and even heroic when resistance entailed the last penalty, was yet in defiance of the law of the land. And, to take this particular case of Glastonbury, it is often stated, that when insisting on its surrender the king was only requiring that to be given up into his hands which Parliament had already conferred on

him. However common the impression, it is
false. What the act (27 Hen. VIII., cap. 28)
of February, 1536, did was to give to the king
and his heirs such monasteries only as were
under the yearly value of £200, or such as
should within a "year next after the making
of" the act "be given or granted to his
majesty by any abbot," &c. So far, therefore,
from handing over to the king the property
of all the monasteries, Parliament distinctly
recognised, at least in the case of all save the
lesser religious houses, the rights of their then
owners, and contemplated their passing to the
king's hands only by the voluntary cession of
the actual possessors. How any surrender
was to be brought about was left to the king
and Crumwell, and the minions on whose
devices there is no need to dwell. Before a
recalcitrant superior, who would yield neither
to blandishments, bribery nor threats, the king,
so far as the act would help him, was powerless.

For this case, however, provision was made,
though but indirectly, in the act of April, 1539
(31 Hen. VIII., cap. 13). This act, which
included a retrospective clause covering the

illegal suppression of the greater monasteries
which had already passed into the king's hands,
granted to Henry all monasteries, &c., which
shall hereafter happen to be dissolved, suppressed, renounced, relinquished, forfeited,
given up or come unto the king's highness.
These terms seem wide enough, but there is
also an ominous parenthesis referring to such
other religious houses as "shall happen to
come to the king's highness by attainder or
attainders *of treason.*"   The clause did not
find its way into the act unawares.   It will be
seen that it was Crumwell's care how and in
whose case the clause should become operative.
And with just so much of countenance as is
thus given him by the act, with the king to
back him, the monasteries of Glastonbury,
Reading and Colchester, from which no surrender could be obtained, "were, against every
principle of received law, held to fall by the
attainder of their abbots for high treason."[1]

---

[1] Hallam, *Constitutional Hist.*, i., 72. Harpsfield, *Pretended
Divorce*, ed. Pocock (Camden Society), p. 300, says : "Such
as would voluntarily give over were rewarded with large annual

The very existence of the clause is, moreover, evidence that by this time Crumwell
knew that among the superiors of the few
monasteries yet standing, there were men with
whom, if the king was not to be baulked of
his intent, the last conclusions would have to
be tried.   To him the necessity would have
been paramount, by every means in his power,
to sweep away what he rightly regarded as
the strongholds of the papal power in the
country, and to get rid of these "spies of the
pope."[1]   Such unnatural enemies of their
prince and gracious lord would fittingly be
first singled out, that their fate might serve as
a warning to other intending evil-doers.   Perhaps, too, Whiting's repute for blamelessness
of life, the discipline which he was known to
maintain in his monastery and his great terri-
torial influence may all have conduced to point
him out as an eminently proper subject to
proceed against, as tending to show the nation

pensions, and with other pleasures.   Against some other there
were found quarrels, as against Hugh Farindon, Abbot of
Reading . . . against Richard Whiting, Abbot of Glaston, &c."
    [1] R. O. *Crumwell Correspondence*, xv., No. 7.

that where the crime of resistance to the king's will was concerned there could be no such thing as an extenuating circumstance, no consideration which would avail to mitigate the penalty.

CHAPTER VI.

THE BEGINNING OF THE END.

IN the story of what follows we are continually hampered by the singularly defective nature of the various records relating to the closing years of Crumwell's administration. We are therefore frequently left to supply links by conjectures, but conjectures in which, from the known facts and such documentary evidence as remains, there is sufficient assurance of being in the main correct.

Already, in 1538, rumour had spoken of the coming dissolution; and the fact that all over the country even the greatest houses of religion, one after another, were falling into the king's hands by surrender, voluntary or enforced, tended to give colour to the current tales. Henry's agents, it is true, had en-

deavoured to dissemble any royal intention of
a general suppression of the monastic body.
They not only denied boldly and unblushingly
that the king had any such design, but urged
upon Crumwell the advisability of putting a
stop to the persistent reports on this subject.
The far-seeing minister, fully alive to the
danger, drafted a letter to reassure the religious
superiors, and dispatched it probably in the
first instance to Glastonbury.[1]

" Albeit," this letter runs, " I doubt not but
(having not long since received the King's
highness's letters wherein his majesty signified
to you that using yourselves like his good and
faithful subjects, his grace would not in any
wise interrupt you in your state and kind of
living ; and that his pleasure therefore was that
in case any man should declare anything to the
contrary you should cause him to be appre-
hended and kept in sure custody till further

---

[1] The previous letter in the Cotton MS. Cleopatra E. iv. is
endorsed : "The mynute of a letter drawn by Mr. Moryson
to th'Abbot of Glastonbury." This endorsement is certainly
wrong ; but Mr. Gairdner (*Calendar* xiii., No. 573 *note*) thinks
the letters may possibly have always been together and the
endorsement refers to the second.

knowledge of his grace's pleasure), you would
so firmly repose yourself in the tenour of the
said letters as no man's words, nor any voluntary surrender made by any governor or company of any religious house since that time,
shall put you in any doubt or fear of suppression
or change of your kind of life and policy."
The king, however, feels that there are people
who " upon any voluntary and frank surrender,
would persuade and blow abroad a general and
violent suppression ;" and, because some houses
have lately been surrendered, the king commands
me to say " that unless there had been over-
tures made by the said houses that have resigned, his grace would never have received the
same, and his majesty intendeth not in any wise
to trouble you or to desire for the suppression
of any house that standeth, except they shall
either desire of themselves with one whole
consent to resign and forsake the same, or else
misuse themselves contrary to their allegiance."
In this last case, the document concludes, they
shall lose " more than their houses and possessions, that is the loss also of their lives."
Wherefore take care of your houses and beware

of spoiling them, like some have done "who imagined they were going to be dissolved."[1]

This letter could scarcely have done much to reassure Abbot Whiting as to the king's real intentions, in view of the obvious facts which each day made them clearer. By the beginning of 1539, Glastonbury was the only religious house left standing in the whole county of Somerset. Rumours must have reached the abbey of the fall of Bath and Keynsham, shortly after the Christmas of the previous year, and of strange methods to which Crumwell's agents had resorted in order to gain possession of Hinton Charterhouse and Benedictine Athelney. At the former, the determination of the monks to hold to their house was apparently in the end broken down by a resort to a rigid examination of the religious on the dangerous royal-supremacy question, which resulted in one of their number being put in prison for "affirming the Bishop of Rome to be Vicar of Christ, and that he ought to be taken for head of the church."

---

[1] B. Mus. Cott. MS. Cleop. E. iv., f. 68.

This of itself must have prepared the mind of Abbot Whiting for the final issue which would have to be faced.

The short respite granted before conclusions were tried with him, could have been to all at Glastonbury little less than a long-drawn suspense, during which the abbot possessed his soul in peace, attending cheerfully to the daily calls of duty. They were left in no doubt as to the real meaning of a dissolution and had witnessed the immediate results which followed upon it. The rude dismantling of churches and cloisters, the rapid sales of vestments and other effects, the pulling down of the lead from roofs and gutters, and the breaking up of bells had gone on all around them; whilst homeless monks and the poor who had from time immemorial found relief in their necessities at religious houses now swept away must have all crowded to Glastonbury during the last few months of its existence. For eleven weeks the royal wreckers, like a swarm of locusts, wandered over Somerset, "defacing, destroying and prostrating the churches, cloisters, belfreys,

and other buildings of the late monasteries ; "
and the roads were worn with carts carrying
away the lead melted from the roofs, barrels
of broken bell-metal, and other plunder.

It was not till the autumn of the year
1539, that any final steps began to be taken
with regard to Glastonbury and its venerable
abbot. Among Crumwell's " remembrances,"
still extant in his own handwriting, of things
to do, or matters to speak about to the king,
in the beginning of September this year occurs
the following :—" Item, for proceeding against
the abbots of Reading, Glaston and the other,
in their own countries."[1]   From this it is clear
that some time between the passing of the act
giving to the crown the possession of all
dissolved or surrendered monasteries, which
came into force in April, 1539, and the September of this year, these abbots must have
been sounded, and it had been found that
compliance in regard of a surrender was not
to be expected.[2]   By the sixteenth of the latter

---

[1] B. Mus. Cott. MS. Titus, B. i., f. 446a.

[2] In the spring of the year, Glastonbury, in common with
other churches in England, was relieved of what it pleased the

month Crumwell's design had been communicated to his familiar Layton, and had elicited from him a reply in which he abjectly asks pardon for having praised the abbot at the time of the visitation. "The Abbot of Glastonbury," he adds, "appeareth neither then nor now to have known God, nor his prince, nor any part of a good Christian man's religion."[1]

Three days later, on Friday, September 19, the royal commissioners, Layton, Pollard and Moyle, suddenly arrived at Glastonbury about ten o'clock in the morning. The abbot had not been warned of their intended visit, and was then at his grange of Sharpham, about a

---

king to consider its "superfluous plate." Pollard, Tregonwell and Petre on May 2nd, 1539, handed to Sir John Williams, the keeper of the royal treasure-house, 493 ounces of gold, 16,000 ounces of gilt plate and 28,700 ounces of parcel gilt and silver plate taken from the monasteries in the west of England. In this amount was included the superfluous plate of Glastonbury. Besides this weight of gold and silver there was placed in the treasury "two collets of gold wherein standeth two coarse emeralds ; a cross of silver gilt, garnished with a great coarse emerald, two 'balaces' and two sapphires, lacking a knob at one of the ends of the same cross ; a superaltar garnished with silver gilt and part gold, called the great sapphire of Glastonbury ; a great piece of unicorn's horn, a piece of mother of pearl like a shell, eight branches of coral " (Monastic Treasures, Abbotsford Club, p. 24).

[1] Ellis, *Original Letters*, 3rd Series, iii., p. 247.

mile from the monastery. Thither they hurried "without delay," and after telling him their purpose examined him at once "upon certain

REMAINS AT SHARPHAM OF THE GRANGE OF THE ABBOTS OF GLASTONBURY.

articles, and for that his answer was not then to our purpose," they say; "we advised him to call to his remembrance that which he had forgotten, and so declare the truth."[1]   Then

---

[1] The whole of this account is from the letter of the commissioners to Crumwell, in Wright, p. 255.

they at once took him back to the abbey, and
when night came on proceeded to search the
abbot's papers and ransack his apartments
" for letters and books, and found in his study,
secretly laid, as well a written book of arguments against the divorce of the king's majesty
and the lady dowager, which we take to be a
great matter, as also divers pardons, copies of
bulls, and the counterfeit life of Thomas Becket
in print ; but we could not," they write, " find
any letter that was material."

Furnished, however, with these pieces of
evidence as to the tendency of Whiting's mind,
the inquisitors proceeded further to examine
him concerning the "articles received from
your lordship" (Crumwell).   In his answers
appeared, they considered, "his cankered and
traitorous mind against the king's majesty and
his succession."   To these replies he signed
his name, "and so with as fair words as " they
could, " being but a very weak man and
sickly," they forthwith sent him up to London
to the Tower, that Crumwell might examine
him for himself.

The rest of the letter is significant for the

eventual purpose they knew their master would regard as of primary importance :—

"As yet we have neither discharged servant nor monk ; but now, the abbot being gone, we will, with as much celerity as we may, proceed to the dispatching of them. We have in money £300 and above ; but the certainty of plate and other stuff there as yet we know not, for we have not had opportunity for the same ; whereof we shall ascertain your lordship so shortly as we may. This is also to advertise your lordship that we have found a fair chalice of gold, and divers other parcels of plate, which the abbot had hid secretly from all such commissioners as have been there in times past ; and as yet he knoweth not that we have found the same ; whereby we think that he thought to make his hand by his untruth to his king's majesty."

A week later, on September 28th,[1] they again write to Crumwell that they "have daily found and tried out both money and plate," hidden in secret places in the abbey, and conveyed for

---

[1] Wright, p. 257.

safety to the country.   They could not tell him
how much they had so far discovered, but it
was sufficient, they thought, to have " begun a
new abbey," and they concluded by asking
what the king wished to have done in respect
of the two monks who were the treasurers of
the church, and the two lay clerks of the
sacristy, who were chiefly to be held respon-
sible in the matter.

On the 2nd October the inquisitors write
again to their master to say that they have
come to the knowledge of " divers and sundry
treasons" committed by Abbot Whiting, " the
certainty whereof shall appear unto your lordship in a book herein enclosed, with the
accusers' names put to the same, which we
think to be very high and rank treasons."   The
original letter, preserved in the Record Office,
clearly shows by the creases in the soiled
yellow paper that some small book or folded
papers have been enclosed.   Whatever it was,
it is no longer forthcoming.   Just at the critical
moment we are again deprived, therefore, of a
most interesting and important source of information.   In view, however, of the common

sufferings of these abbots, who were dealt with
together, the common fate which befel them,
and the common cause assigned by contemporary writers for their death,—viz., their attainder
"of high treason for denying the king to be
supreme head of the Church," as Hall, the
contemporary London lawyer (who reports
what must have been current in the capital),
phrases it—there can be no doubt that these
depositions were much of the same nature as
those made against Thomas Marshall, Abbot of
Colchester, to which subsequent reference will
be made. It is certain that with Abbot Whiting in the Tower and Crumwell's commissioners engaged in "dispatching" the monks
"with as much celerity" as possible, Glastonbury was already regarded as part of the royal
possessions. Even before any condemnation
the matter is taken as settled, and on October
the 24th, 1539, Pollard handed over to the
royal treasurer the riches still left at the abbey
as among the possessions of "attainted persons
and places."[1]

---

[1] *Monastic Treasures* (Abbotsford Club), p. 38. These con-
sisted of 71 ozs. of gold with stones, 7,214 ozs. of gilt plate, and
6,387 ozs. of silver.

Whilst Layton and his fellows were rummaging at Glastonbury, Abbot Whiting was safely lodged in the Tower of London. There he was subjected to searching examinations. A note in Crumwell's own hand, entered in his "remembrances," says :

"Item. Certain persons to be sent to the Tower for the further examination of the Abbot of Glaston."[1]

At this time it was supposed that Parliament, which ought to have met on November 1st of this year, would be called upon to consider the charges against the abbot. At least Marillac, the French ambassador, who shows that he was always well informed on public matters writes to his master that this is to be done. Even when the assembly was delayed till the arrival of the king's new wife, Ann of Cleves, the ambassador repeats that the decision of Whiting's case will now be put off. He adds that "they have found a manuscript in favour of queen Catherine, and against the marriage of queen Anne, who was afterwards beheaded,"

---

[1] B. Mus. Cott., MS. Titus, B. i., f. 441 *a*.

which is objected against the abbot.[1] Poor
Catherine had been at rest in her grave for
four years, and her rival in the affections of
Henry had died on the scaffold nearly as many
years, before Layton and his fellow-inquisitors
found the written book of arguments in
Whiting's study, and "took it to be a great
matter" against him. It is hardly likely that,
even if more loyal to Catherine's memory than
there is any possible reason to suppose, Whiting
would stick at a point where More and Fisher
could yield, and would not have given his ad-
hesion to the succession as settled by Parliament. But as in their case, it was the thorny
questions which surrounded the divorce, the
subject all perilous of "treason," which brought
him at last, as it brought them first, to the
scaffold.

It is more than strange that the ordinary procedure was not carried out in this case. According to all law, Abbot Whiting and the
Abbots of Reading and Colchester should have
been arraigned before Parliament, as they were

---

[1] Kaulek, *Inventaire Analytique, ut sup.*, No. 161.

members of the House of Peers, but no such
bill of attainder was ever presented, and in
fact the execution had taken place before the
Parliament came together.[1]

The truth is, that Abbot Whiting and the
others were condemned to death as the result
of secret inquisitions in the Tower. Crumwell,
acting as "prosecutor, judge and jury,"[2] had
really arranged for their execution before they
left their prison. What happened in the case
of Abbot Whiting at Wells, and in that of
Abbot Cook at Reading, was but a ghastly
mockery of justice, enacted merely to cover the
illegal and iniquitous proceedings which had

---

[1] According to Wriothesley's *Chronicle* they were arraigned
in the "Counter." "Also in this month [November] the abbates
of Glastonburie, Reding and Colchester were arrayned in the
Counter." It is worthy of notice that whilst all trace or record
of a trial has disappeared, the legal records are explicit as to a
point of fact. Of course the king could only obtain the possessions of the monastery by the attainder of the abbot for high
treason, and accordingly the official documents all speak of the
attainder for high treason. For instance L. T. R. Memoranda
Roll, 32 Henry VIII., m. 2, has : "Omnes libertates &c. dicti
nuper abbatis Glaston sunt in manu dicti Regis nunc ratione
attincturæ præfati abbatis qui nuper de alta prodicione attinctus
fuit." These presentments in the Counter or at Wells were
evidently empty shows, intended to impress the populace.

[2] Froude, *Hist.*, iii., p. 432.

7

FACSIMILE OF PART OF CRUMWELL'S "REMEMBRANCES,"
COTTON MS., TITUS B. I. f. 441a.

condemned them untried. This Crumwell has
written down with his own hand. He notes in
his " remembrances " :—[1]

Item. Councillors to give evidence against the abbot
of Glaston, Richard Pollard, Lewis Forstell and Thomas
Moyle. Item. To see that the evidence be *well sorted*
and the indictments *well drawn* against the said abbots
and their accomplices. Item. How the king's learned
counsel shall be with me all this day, for the full conclusion of the indictments.

And then, to sum up all :—

Item. The Abbot of Glaston to be *tried* at Glaston,
and *also executed* there.[2]

As Crumwell was so solicitous about the
fate of the abbots as to devote the whole of
one of his precious days to the final settle-
ment of their case, in later times no less
great was the solicitude of his panegyrist,

---

[1] *Ut sup.*, ff. 441 *a* and *b*.

[2] The following is a transcript of the passages contained in
the facsimile opposite. " Item certayn persons to be sent to
the Towre for the further examenacyon of the abbot of Glaston.
Item letters to be sent with the copye of the judgement ageynst
Sir John Sayntlow's men for the rape and burgalrye don in
Somersetshyre unto lorde presedent Russell with a streyt com-
mandement to procede to justyce. Item the abbot Redyng
to be sent down to be tryed and executyd at Reding with his
complycys. Item the abbot of Glaston to tryed at Glaston
and also executyd there with his complycys."

Burnet, to "discover the impudence of Sanders" in saying they suffered for denying the king's supremacy, and to prove that they did not. Even at a time when records were not so accessible as they now are, Collier, Burnet's contemporary, could see clearly enough where lay the truth. "What the particulars were (of the abbots' attainder) our learned Church historian (Burnet) confesses 'he can't tell; for the record of their attainders is lost.' But, as he goes on, 'some of our own writers (Hall, Grafton) deserve a severe censure, who write it was for denying, &c., the king's supremacy. Whereas, if they had not undertaken to write the history without any information at all, they must have seen that the whole clergy, and especially the abbots, had over and over again acknowledged the king's supremacy.' But how does it appear our historians are mistaken? Has this gentleman seen the Abbot of Colchester's indictment or perused his record of attainder? He confesses no. How then is his censure made good? He offers no argument beyond conjecture. He concludes the Abbot of Colchester had formerly acknowledged the king's supremacy, and from thence infers he could not suffer now for denying it. But do not people's opinions alter sometimes, and conscience and courage improve? Did not Bishop Fisher and Cardinal Pool, at least as this author represents them, acknowledge the king's supremacy at first? And yet it is certain they afterwards showed themselves of another mind to a very remarkable degree. . . . Farther, does not himself tell us that many of the Carthusians were executed for their open denying the king's supremacy, and why then might not some of the abbots have the same belief and fortitude with others of their fraternity?" (*Eccl. Hist.*, ii., 173.) The real way of reaching them was through conscience, a way which, as we have seen, had just before been tried in the case of the Abbot Whiting's near neighbours, the Carthusians of Hinton. "To reach the abbots, therefore," continues Collier," that other way, the oath of supremacy was offered them, and upon their refusal they were condemned for high treason (p. 164).

But amidst these cares Crumwell never for-

got the king's business, the "great matter," the
end which this iniquity was to compass.   With
the prize now fairly within his grasp, he
notes :—

> The plate of Glastonbury, 11,000 ounces and over,
> besides golden.   The furniture of the house of Glaston.
> In ready money from Glaston, £1,100 and over.   The
> rich copes from Glaston.   The whole year's revenue of
> Glaston.   The debts of Glaston, £2,000 and above.[1]

Layton has borne witness to the state of
spirituals in Glastonbury ; Crumwell gives final
testimony to the abbot's good administration of
temporals.   The house by this time had,
according to Crumwell's construction, come to
the king's highness by attainder of treason.   It
remained now to inaugurate the line of policy
on which Elizabeth improved later, and after,
in the secret tribunal of the Tower, condemn-
ing the abbot without trial for cause of conscience in a sentence that involved forfeiture
of life and goods, to put him to death, so Lord
Russell says, as if for common felony, the "rob-
bing of Glastonbury Church."

---

[1] *Ibid.*, f. 446 *a.*   The debts named here were evidently due
to Glastonbury.

And now it only remains to follow the venerable man on his pilgrimage to the scene of his martyrdom.[1]

As we have seen under Crumwell's hand, Abbot Whiting's fate was already settled before he left the Tower. In the interrogatories, preliminary but decisive, which he had there undergone, the abbot had come face to face with the inevitable issue. He knew to what end the way through the Tower had, from the

---

[1] The original edition of Sander simply says that the three abbots and the two priests, Rugg and Onion, "ob negatam Henrici pontificiam potestatem martyrii coronam adepti sunt." In the second and later editions this is cut out, another reason is assigned for their death, and an obviously legendary narrative about Whiting is inserted in the text. It is impossible to credit many of these oft-repeated statements. They seem to embody the gossip of half a century later; in some points running near enough to the truth, in others partaking of legend; such as the sensational scene, wanting alike in sense and probability, in the hall of the palace on the abbot's arrival at Wells; the assembly prepared to receive him, his proceeding to take the place of honour among the first, the unexpected summons to stand down and answer to the charge of treason, the old man's wondering inquiry what this meant, the whispered assurance that it was all a matter of form to strike terror—into whom or wherefore the story does not tell. These and later details are here entirely thrown aside, since they cannot be reconciled with the official documents of the time and private letters of the persons engaged in the act itself.

time of More and Fisher to his own hour, led those who had no other satisfaction to give the king than that which he could offer.

It is not impossible, however, that hopes may have been held out to him that in his extreme old age and weakness of body he might be spared extremities ; this supposition seems to receive some countenance from the narrative given below. But Henry and Crumwell had determined that Abbot Whiting should suffer before all the world the last indignity. And they designed for him the horrible death of a traitor in the sight of his own subjects who had known and loved him for many years, on the scene of his own former greatness.

The following extract from an unknown but contemporary writer, in giving the only details of the journey homeward that are known to exist, manifests the abbot's characteristic simplicity and perfect possession of soul in patience, together with a real sense of what the end would certainly be.

Going homewards to Glastonbury, the abbot had one Pollard appointed to wait upon him, who was an especial favourer of Crumwell, whom the abbot neither desired

to accompany him, neither yet dared to refuse him. At
the next bait, when the abbot went to wash, he desired
Mr. Pollard to come wash with him, who by no means
would be entreated thereunto. The abbot seeing such
civility, mistrusted so much the more such courtesy was
not void of some subtility, and said unto him : " Mr.
Pollard, if you be to me a companion, I pray you wash
with me and sit down ; but if you be my keeper and I your
prisoner, tell me plainly, that I may prepare my mind to
to go to another room better fitting my fortunes. And
if you be neither, I shall be content to ride without your
company." Whereupon Pollard protested that he did
forbear to do what the abbot desired him only in respect
of the reverence he bore his age and virtues, and that
he was appointed by those in authority to bear him
company of worship's sake, and therefore might not
forsake him till he did see him safe at Glastonbury.

Notwithstanding all this, the abbot doubted somewhat,
and told one (Thomas) Horne, whom he had brought up
from a child, that he misdoubted (him) somewhat, Judas
having betrayed his master. And yet though (Horne)
were both privy and plotter of his master's fall, yet did
he sweare most intolerably he knew of no harm towards
him, neither should any be done to him as long as he
was in his company ; wishing besides that the devil
might have him if he were otherwise than he told him.
But before he came to Glastonbury, Horne forsook,
and joined himself unto his enemies.[1]

---

[1] B. Mus. Sloane MS. 2495. The passage in the text is taken
from an early seventeenth-century life of Henry VIII. It is,
however, a free translation of Arundel MS., 151, No. 62, which
is a hitherto unnoticed account of the divorce, written somewhere
about the year 1557, and dedicated to Philip and Mary. Some of

CHAPTER VII.

THE MARTYRDOM.

THE venerable abbot thus journeyed home
in the company of Pollard. It was this
Pollard who had been Crumwell's agent in
sending him to the Tower, who had weeks ago
turned the monks out of the monastery and
had begun the wrecking of Glastonbury Abbey,
a house, which on his first arrival there he had
described to his employer as "great, goodly
and so princely that we have not seen the like;"
and in another letter he repeats the same assurance, adding that "it is a house meet for the
king's majesty, and for no one else."[1]

the details agree with those given about Whiting by Le Grand
(*Défense*, iii., p. 210), who may have drawn them from the
same source.
[1] Wright, *Suppression of the Monasteries*, pp. 256, 258.

Measures had already been taken to have all
secure at Wells, although Abbot Whiting had
evidently been left in ignorance of the fact that
there was now no Glastonbury Abbey for him
to return to. Crumwell's captive reached Wells
on Friday, November 14, and once safely
brought back into his own country there was
neither delay nor dissembling. The plan
devised was rushed through without giving
a soul among the unhappy actors in the
scene time to reflect upon what they were
doing—time to recover their better selves—
time to avert the guilt which in some measure
must fall upon them. In accordance with the
wicked policy so often pursued in Tudor times,
a jury—the people themselves—were made
active agents in accomplishing the royal vengeance, the execution of which had been
already irrevocably settled in London. John,
Lord Russell, had for some time past been
superintending the necessary arrangements in
the county of Somerset itself. His business
had been to get together a jury which he could
trust to do, or perhaps in this case tacitly countenance, the king's will, and it was one part of

his care, when all was over, to send to Crumwell
their names with a view, doubtless, of securing
their due reward.   Unfortunately, although
Russell's letter is preserved the list enclosed has
perished.   But a letter from Pollard to Crumwell gives the names of some who distinguished
themselves by their zeal, and who had been
" very diligent to serve the king at this time."
Among these first of all is " my brother Paulet,"
for whom is bespoken " the surveyorship of
Glaston," with the promise to Crumwell that
" his lordship's goodness," showed in this
matter, Paulet when he takes the prize " shall
recompense to his little power."   Other diligent persons whom Pollard specially names are
John Sydenham and Thomas Horner, and
finally Nicholas FitzJames, the same who, but
a year or two before, had written to Crumwell
in Abbot Whiting's behalf.

As is well known from the history of the
Pilgrimage of Grace, jury-making had at this
time been raised to an art,—an art so exquisitely
refined that it aimed at making friends, kins-
folk, even brothers the accomplices by word of
mouth in the legal or illegal murders which

disgraced this reign. The minds of the men selected in this case to register the decrees of the kingly omnipotence, escape our means of inquiry, but Lord Russell has recorded "that they formed as worshipful a jury as were found here these many years," and of this fact he "ensured" his "good lord" Crumwell.

Russell's care, moreover, had been diligently exercised, not merely in assembling the jury, but in getting together an audience for the occasion. His efforts were successful, for he gathered at Wells such a concourse of people, that he was able to declare "there was never seen in these parts so great appearance as were here at this present time." He adds the assurance so tediously common in documents of that pre-eminently courtly age, that none had ever been seen "better willing to serve the king."[1]

This was the scene which met Abbot Whiting's eyes in Pollard's company as he entered the city of Wells, where so often before he had been received as a venerated and honoured

---

[1] Wright, *Suppression of the Monasteries*, p. 260.

guest. Unfortunately we have no direct and continuous narrative of all that took place. If it was dangerous to speak it was still more dangerous to write in those days, except of course in one sense,—that which was pleasing to the court. Fortunately two letters survive, written by the chief managers of the business, John, Lord Russell, and Richard Pollard, one of the "counsel" who had been engaged in the Tower with Crumwell, for the careful drawing of the indictment against the abbot. Both were written on the Sunday, the day following the execution. An earlier letter by Pollard, written on the day itself and evidently giving more details, is wanting in the vast mass of Crumwell's papers. This, the earliest news of the accomplishment of the king's will, was not improbably taken by the ready minister to the king himself and left with his majesty. Fragmentary though the records that exist are, and only giving here a hint, there a mere outline of what took place, without order and without sequence, they in this form have a freshness and truthfulness which still enable us to realise what actually took place.

RUINS OF THE HALL OF THE BISHOP'S PALACE AT WELLS, SAID TO HAVE BEEN THE COURT WHERE THE PROCEEDINGS TOOK PLACE.

Face p. 111.

On the abbot's arrival in the city of Wells, the business was begun without waiting to give the condemned man time for rest or for thought. Pollard was in charge of the indictment, over which Crumwell had spent his day, in the drafting of which so many counsel learned in the law had exercised their ingenuity, and which was the outcome of the secret examinations conducted during the abbot's two months' imprisonment in the Tower. But it was by no means intended that a drop of bitterness in the cup should be spared him; every successive stage of indignity was to be offered the venerable man till his last breath and then to his lifeless body. He was to be struck in the house of his friends, and by his own dependents. From out the crowd there came forward new accusers, "his tenants and others," putting up "many accusations for wrongs and injuries he had done them:" not of course that it was in the least intended that there should be time for enquiry into their truth; the mere accusations were enough, and they were part of the drama that had been elaborated with such care.

But this was not the only business of the
day. The venerable man was to be asso-
ciated and numbered with a rabble of common
felons, and to stand in the same rank with
them. Together with the abbot of the great
monastery of Glastonbury there were a number
of people of the lowest class—how many we
know not—who were accused of "rape and
burglary." "They were all condemned," says
Russell, and four of them "the next day, if not
the same day, put to execution at the place of
the act done, which is called the Mere, and
there adjudged to hang still in chains to the
example of others."

Of any verdict or of any condemnation of
the abbot and of his two monks nothing is said
by Russell or Pollard, but they proceed at once
to the execution.[1]

It is not impossible, seeing the rapid way in
which the whole business was carried through,

---

[1] After a careful consideration of the evidence, my belief is
that there was no trial of the abbot and his two companions
at Wells. The sentence passed on them in London was probably published to the jury there, but there is nothing to show
that it was asked to find any verdict.

that had the scene of the so-called trial been
Glastonbury in place of Wells, the abbot would
have met his fate and gained his crown that
very day. But the king and his faithful
minister, Crumwell, had devised in the town of
Glastonbury a scene which was to be more
impressive than that which had taken place in
the neighbouring city, more calculated to strike
terror into the hearts of the old man's friends
and followers.

After being pestered by Pollard with "divers
articles and interrogatories," the result of which
was that he would accuse no man but himself,
nor "confess no more gold nor silver, nor anything more than he did before you [Crumwell]
in the Tower," the next morning, Saturday,
November 15,[1] the venerable abbot with his
two monks, John Thorne and Roger James,
were delivered over to the servants of Pollard

---

[1] It is generally stated that the martyrdom took place on
November 14. The authority for this is a statement in the
original edition of Sander, that the three abbots obtained the
crown of martyrdom "ad decimum octavum kalendas Decem-
bris." Mr. David Lewis in his translation has not noticed the
error. It is certain from the original letters of Pollard and
Russell that the true date is Saturday, November 15.

8

for the performance of what more had to be
done.   Under this escort they were carried
from Wells to Glastonbury.   Arrived at the
entrance of the town the abbot was made to
dismount.   And now all the brutal indignities
and cruel sufferings attending the death of a
traitor condemned for treason were inflicted
upon him.   And in truth, like many a true
and noble Englishman of that day, Richard
Whiting was, in the sense of Crumwell and
Henry, a traitor to his king.   The case from
their point of view is well expressed by one
of the truculent preachers patronised by the
sovereign as his most fitting apologists.

"For had not Richard[1] Whiting, that was
Abbot of Glastonbury, trow ye, great cause, all
things considered, to play so traitorous a part
as he hath played, whom the king's highness
made of a vile, beggarly, monkish merchant,
governor and ruler of seven thousand marks
by the year?   Trow ye this was not a good
pot of wine?   Was not this a fair almose at
one man's door?   Such a gift had been worth

---

[1] The name in the MS. is John, but it is evidently a mistake.

GENERAL VIEW OF GLASTONBURY TOR.

Face p. 114.

grammercy to many a man. But Richard
Whiting having always a more desirous eye to
treason than to truth, careless, laid apart both
God's goodness and the king's, and stuck hard
by the Bishop of Rome and the Abbot of
Reading in the quarrel of the Romish Church.
Alas! what a stony heart had (Richard) Whit-
ing, to be so unkind to so loving and benefi-
cent a prince, and so false a traitor to Henry
VIII., king of his native country, and so true,
I say, to that cormorant of Rome."

In this new meaning of treason, Abbot
Whiting was adjudged the traitor's death. At
the outskirts of his own town his venerable
limbs were extended on a hurdle, to which a
horse was attached. In this way he was
dragged on that bleak November morning
along the rough hard ground through the
streets of Glastonbury, of which he and his
predecessors had so long been the loved and
honoured lords and masters. It was thus
among his own people that, now at the age
of well nigh fourscore years, Abbot Whiting
made his last pilgrimage through England's
"*Roma Secunda.*" As a traitor for conscience
sake he was drawn past the glorious monas-

tery, now desolate and deserted, past the
great church, that home of the saints and
whilom sanctuary of this country's greatness,
now devastated and desecrated, its relics of
God's holy ones dispersed, its tombs of kings
dishonoured, on further still to the summit of
that hill which rises yet in the landscape in
solitary and majestic greatness, the perpetual
memorial of the deed now to be enacted.[1]
For, thanks to the tenacity with which the
memory of "good Abbot Whiting" has been
treasured by generations of the townsfolk,

[1] It has been suggested that the place of Abbot Whiting's
martyrdom was not the Tor, but a smaller hill nearer the town,
called Chalice Hill. The ground of this supposition is that the
site of the abbey is not visible from the Tor, whilst it is from the
latter hill. The steps by which the conclusion was arrived
at that this consequently was the place of martyrdom, would
appear to be the following : (1) Sander, in the original edition
of the *Schism*, states that the abbot was executed on the Tor.
(2) The Roman editor makes on this an explanatory addition,
perfectly reasonable when writing for persons who were not
acquainted with Glastonbury. The execution took place, he
says, *ad montis editi cacumen qui monasterio imminet, i.e.*, over-
hangs, that is, *rises above* the monastery. This has been taken
in the sense of *overlooking*, and next "overlook" in its strictest
sense, as implying that the abbey was visible from the place
of execution. It is only necessary, in order to refute a theory
having no better basis than inaccuracy and misunderstanding,
to refer to the simple assertion of the persons engaged in the
execution of Abbot Whiting, who wrote at the very time it was
taking place, and who knew perfectly well what Tor hill was.

the very hill to-day is Abbot Whiting's monument.

His last act was simple. Now about to appear before a tribunal that was searching, just

SUMMIT OF TOR HILL.

and merciful, he asks forgiveness first of God and then of man, even of those who had most offended against justice in his person and had

not rested until they had brought him to the
gallows amidst every incident that could add
to such a death—ignominy and shame.   The
venerable abbot remains to the last the same
as he always appears throughout his career;
suffering in self-possession and patience the
worst that man could inflict upon his mortal
body, in the firm assurance that in all this he
was but following in the footsteps of that Lord
and Master in whose service from his youth
upwards he had spent his life.

In this supreme moment his two monks,
John Thorne[1] and Roger James,[2] the one a

----

[1] A comparison of the lists of monks qualified to take part in
the election of Abbot Whiting in 1523 and the list appended to
the acknowledgment of supremacy in 1534 seems to show that
John Arthur, *treasurer* in 1523, is identical with *John Thorne*,
treasurer in 1539, martyred with Abbot Whiting.   This comparison also shows that the maker of the chair figured at p. 60,
can be no other than *John Thorne*, the martyr.   The lists of
monks give only the Christian name and the name in religion
(in this case Arthur).   In the legal proceedings, for the religious
name the family name, Thorne, is substituted.

The lists of 1523 and 1534 are noteworthy as showing how
keen was the interest taken by the Glastonbury monks in the
past of their house.   Amongst the religious names occur :
Abaramathea, Joseph, Arthur, Derivian, Gildas, Benen, Aidan,
Ceolfrid, Indractus, Aldhelm, Dunstan, Ethelwold, Edgar,
and other saints connected with Glastonbury.

[2] Roger James is evidently identical with Roger Wilfrid, who
in the list of 1534 was the youngest monk of the house.

PORTRAIT OF JOHN THORNE, IN THE POSSESSION OF THE ENGLISH
BENEDICTINES OF ST. EDMUND'S, NOW SETTLED AT DOUAI.
PAINTED IN THE 17TH CENTURY.

Face p. 118.

man of mature age and experience, the other
not long professed, showed themselves worthy
sons of so good a father. They, too, begged
forgiveness of all and "took their death also
very patiently." Even Pollard seems moved
for the moment, for he adds with an un-
wonted touch of tenderness, "whose souls
God pardon."

There is here no need to dwell on the
butchery which followed, and to tell how the
hardly lifeless body was cut down, divided
into four parts and the head struck off. One
quarter was despatched to Wells, another to
Bath, a third to Ilchester, and the fourth to
Bridgewater, whilst the venerable head was
fixed over the great gateway of the abbey,
a ghastly warning of the retribution which
might and would fall on all, even the most
powerful or the most holy, if they ventured
to stand between the king and the accomplishment of his royal will.

All this might indeed strike terror into the
people of the whole country, but not even the
will of a Tudor monarch could prevent the
people from forming their own judgment on

the deed that had been done, and preserving,
although robbed of the Catholic faith, the
memory of the "good Abbot Whiting." It
is easy to understand how, so soon after the
event as Mary's reign, the inhabitants of the
town and neighbourhood, with a vivid recollec-
tion of the past, were ready and even eager to
make personal sacrifices for the restoration of
the abbey.   But even a hundred years later,
and indeed even down to the present day, the
name of Abbot Whiting has been preserved
as a household word at Glastonbury and in its
neighbourhood.   There are those living who,
when conversing with aged poor people, were
touched to find the affectionate reverence with
which his name was still treasured on the spot,
though why he died and what it was all about
they could not tell.   That he was a good, a
kind, a holy man they knew, for they had been
told so in the days of their youth by those
who had gone before.

CHAPTER VIII.

ABBOT HUGH COOK OF READING.

THE abbeys of Reading and Colchester, although of the first rank, seeing that their abbots were peers of Parliament, and Reading certainly among the most distinguished houses of the country, had no such position as that of Glastonbury. They were both Norman creations ; Reading being founded by King Henry II. and chosen by him as his burial place. By favour of its royal founder the commonalty of Reading recognised the abbot as their lord ; the mayor of the city " being the abbot's mayor, &c.," as the diocesan, Bishop Shaxton writes, to Crumwell.

The history of the fall of Reading Abbey and of the execution of Hugh Cook, or Faringdon, the abbot, would be in its main features but a repetition of the story of Glas-

tonbury and Abbot Whiting. The chief
source of information about the Abbot of
Reading is a paper, already referred to, which
is still to be found among the public records,
although it has remained unnoticed till four or
five years ago.[1] It was so decayed with age
as to be almost dropping to pieces, but now
encased in tissue paper it is fortunately legible
almost in its entirety. The document in question is a virulent and brutal invective, evidently
a sermon, drawn up for the approval of Crumwell, to be delivered in justification of the
king's action in putting to death the three
Benedictine abbots and their companions. It
is unlikely that this proposed sermon was ever
delivered, for the deed was done, the abbots
were dead, their property was now all in the
king's hands, and from the point of view of
the authors the less said about the matter
the better. The draft was accordingly thrown
by Crumwell into the vast mass of papers of
all sorts accumulating on his hands, which on
his attainder was seized by the king and transferred, as it stood, to the royal archives.

---

[1] R. O. State Papers, 1539, No. 251.

It seems not improbable that the author of
the paper in question was Latimer. The
harangue is brutal ; it shows all his power of
effective alliteration, and it is written quite in
the spirit of the man who begged to be allowed
to preach at the martyrdom of Blessed John
Forrest, and to be placed near him that he
might with better effect insult him in his death
agonies. It is certainly written by a person
fully acquainted with all the circumstances,
and throws light on many matters which
would be unintelligible without it. The paper
is so far of the highest value ; but in dealing
with its statements it is to be remembered
that the one object of the writer is to blacken
the memory of the martyred abbots, to
degrade them and to bring them by every
means into contempt.

From the account of Abbot Cook's origin
given by this writer, it would be gathered that
he was born in humble circumstances. He
thus apostrophises the abbot after his death :
" Ah, Hugh Cook, Hugh Cook ! nay, Hugh
Scullion rather I may him call that would be
so unthankful to so merciful a prince, so un-

kind to so loving a king, and so traitorous to
so true an emperor. The king's highness of
his charity took Hugh Cook out his cankerous
cloister and made him, being at that time the

ARMS OF ABBOT COOK, FROM MS. L.10 OF THE COLLEGE OF
ARMS, p. 73.

most vilest, the most untowardest and the most
miserablest monk that was in the monastery of
Reading, born to nought else but to an old pair

of beggarly boots, and made him, I say, ruler and governor of three thousand marks by the year." But the testimony of the writer on a point of fact such as this cannot be rated high.

It is probable that Abbot Cook belonged to that class from which the English monastic houses had been so largely recruited, "the devouter and younger children of our nobility and gentry who here had their education and livelihood."[1] There seems to be no doubt that he belonged to a Kentish family known to the heralds.[2] His election to the office of abbot took place in 1520. Grafton and Hall in their chronicles, in accordance with the practice common at the time, to depreciate falsely by any and every means, those who had fallen

---

[1] Bodleian MS. Wood, B. vi. Woodhope's " Book of Obits."

[2] It has been considered doubtful whether the name of the last abbot of Reading was Cook or Faringdon. He is sometimes called by one, sometimes by the other name. In the entry of his conviction for treason upon the Controlment Roll, usually very exact, he is called only by the name of " Cooke." As to the arms borne by the abbot, Cole, the antiquary, writes as follows :—" In a curious MS. Book of Heraldry, on vellum and painted, supposed to (be) written about 1520, contayning all ye arms of Persons who had a chevron in the same, is this entered : Hugh Faringdon, *alias* Cooke, Abbat of Reading. Gules a chevron lozenge sable and argent inter 3 Bezants each

into the disfavour of the reigning tyrant, give him the character of an illiterate person. "The contrary," writes Browne Willis, "will appear to such as will consult his *Epistles to the University of Oxford*, remaining in the register of that university, or shall have an opportunity of perusing a book entitled *The art or craft of Rhetorick*, written by Leonard Cox, schoolmaster of Reading. 'Twas printed in the year 1524, and is dedicated by the author to this abbot. He speaks very worthily and honourably of Faringdon on account of his learning."[1]

charged with a cinquefoil gules, on a chief argent a Dove inter 2 Flowers azure. This book belongs to my Friend Mr. Blomfield of Norwich.—W. C. 1748." (Note in Cole's copy of Browne Willis, *Mitred Abbeys*, i., 161, now in possession of the Earl of Gainsborough.) These arms, impaled with those of Reading Abbey, are also given in Coates' *Reading*, plate vii., engraved with a portrait of the abbot, from a piece of stained glass, formerly in Sir John Davis' chapel at Bere Court near Pangbourne. These are the arms of the family of Cook.

[1] Browne Willis, *Mitred Abbeys*, i., 161. For Leonard Cox consult *Dict. of National Biography*, xii., 136. Cox's preface referred to is printed in Coates' *Reading*. The whole is interesting, but it is too long to quote here. It may be gathered that Cox had been a protégé of the abbot, who bestowed much care in advancing the interest of promising youths, and that Greek was taught as well as Latin in " your grammar schole,

A letter written by Cook to the university in Oxford in 1530 is evidence of the abbot's intelligent zeal for the Catholic religion, which at that time was being attacked by the new heresies springing up on all sides. Among the monks of Reading abbey was one Dom John Holyman, "a most stout champion in his preachings and writings against the Lutherans," who, "desirous of a stricter life had resigned his fellowship at New College, Oxford, and taken the cowl at Reading Abbey." When Holyman was to receive the doctorate, Abbot Cook asked that he might be excused from lecturing before the university, as the custom was, so that he might preach in London, where there was greater need of such a man, seeing that the city was already infected with

founded by your antecessours in this your towne of Redynge." It may be worth while to mention here that in the years 1499 and 1500 a Greek, one John Serbopoulos, of Constantinople, was copying Greek MSS. in Reading. Two of these thick folios written on vellum now form MSS. 23 and 24 in the library of Corpus Christi College, Oxford. They were among Grocyn's books, and came to the college through the instrumentality of John Claymond, who was known and patronised by Abbot Bere, of Glastonbury. Grocyn himself was taught Greek by William Sellyng, Prior of Christ Church, Canterbury (see *Downside Review*, December, 1894).

Lutheranism, and where the great popularity which Holyman already enjoyed brought crowds to hear him whenever he appeared in the pulpit at St. Paul's.

On the visitation of Reading Abbey by Doctor London in 1535, the report was favourable as to the state of discipline. "They have," writes the Doctor, "a good lecture in Scripture daily read in their chapter-house both in English and Latin, to which is good resort, and the abbot is at it himself."[1] It is possible that at this time in the visitors' injunctions as in their report Reading was lightly treated. It must have been known to them, as it evidently was to Crumwell, that the abbot was in high favour with the king.

At any rate this circumstance will explain the sharpness of a correspondence which took place at this time between Shaxton, Bishop of Salisbury, in which diocese Reading was situated, and Crumwell. The latter takes up the very unusual position as defender of an abbot, and administers a sharp reproof to

---

[1] Wright, p. 226.

the bishop for his meddlesome interference
in matters in which, as Crumwell tells him
plainly, he has no concern beyond a desire
to obtain preferment for an unworthy de-
pendent of his own.

It appears that the lecturer in scripture at
the abbey was one Dom Roger London, a
monk of the house. In the usual encouragement given to tale-bearing at this time, some
discontented religious had delated their teacher
to Bishop Shaxton as guilty of heresy. "The
matters were no trifles," says Shaxton, himself
at that time a strong supporter of Lutheranism ;
and the four points of suggested heresy certainly run counter to the teaching of the
German doctor. Shaxton examined him personally, "as favourably as I could do," he
writes, "and found him a man of very small
knowledge and of worse judgment." In the
discussion which followed the bishop failed to
bring the monk to his mind, and this determined him to procure the appointment of a
man after his own heart, one Richard Cobbes,
who had been a priest and canon, but who
was then "a married man and degraded."

9

Shaxton applied to Crumwell for the appointment of Cobbes as lecturer to the monks in Dom Roger London's place "with stipend and commons" at the expense of the monastery.[1]

Crumwell, on receipt of the bishop's letter, wrote to the abbot complaining that "the divinity lecture had not been read in the abbey as it ought to have been," and recommending Cobbes for the post of lecturer. Abbot Cook replied that he had already a fully qualified teacher, "a bachelor of divinity and brother of the house, who, by the judgment of others" better able to judge than himself, was "very learned in both divinity and humanities, profitting the brethren both in the Latin tongue and in Holy Scripture." He concludes by pointing out that this teacher read his lecture at far less charge than a stranger would do, and offers him to be examined by any whom Crumwell might appoint. As to the bishop's nominee, the abbot points out the condition of the man, and naturally

[1] Gairdner, *Calendar*, xiii., i., No. 143 (Jan. 26th, the Abbot of Reading to Crumwell).

declares him to be "a most dangerous man" to hold such a position in the monastery. Under these circumstances Abbot Cook refused to admit Cobbes into his house, and continued his monk, Dom Roger London, in the lecture-ship.

Finding that he had not got his way, Shaxton at once proceeded to inhibit the monk from reading at Reading, and put a stop to the lectures altogether. The bishop had evidently expected that Crumwell would out of hand have appointed Cobbes to the post on his first representation; "the which thing, if it had come to pass, so should I not have needed to have inhibited the said monk his reading; but I bare with him," he writes, "to say his creed, so long as there was hope to have another reader there. But when my expectation was frustrated in that behalf, then was I driven to do that which I was loathe to do and which, nevertheless, I was bound to do."

No one could have been more in sympathy with Shaxton's views on this matter than Crumwell. With the exception of the Arch-bishop of Canterbury and the Bishop of

Worcester—that is, Cranmer, and Latimer—no one was more according to the minister's mind in religious matters than Bishop Shaxton; for all of them were true Lutherans at heart. Two of these prelates, indeed, continued honest in the year 1539 when brought face to face with the king's "Six Articles," which extinguished the immediate hopes of the Lutherans in England. They resigned their sees, whilst Cranmer, in accordance with his guiding principle, sacrificed his convictions and held to his archiepiscopal office.

In the matter of the Reading lectureship Shaxton had counted that his ground was safe; and so indeed it was, up to the one point of that personal caprice which, throughout his reign, Henry maintained as the most cherished point of his royal prerogative. Whatever be the cause or explanation of the bishop's failure in this matter, one thing is clear: Henry had a real affection for the Abbot of Reading, so far as his affection could go, and used, as the contemporary libeller reports, to call him familiarly "his own abbot."

Shaxton was intent on doing his duty as a

good pastor of sound Lutheran principles. But Crumwell had that all-determining and all-varying factor to consider, the king's fancy. He accordingly wrote to the abbot to tell him that he need not pay any attention to the Bishop of Salisbury's inhibition. " I," writes Shaxton on hearing of this, "could not obtain so much of you by word or writing to have your pleasure, and the Abbot of Reading could out of hand get and obtain your letters to hinder me in my right proceeding towards his just correction." Beyond this, not merely was the bishop's action set aside, but he had to submit to such a lecture from the king's vicar-general as may have decided him to resign his office when a few months later the " Six Articles " came to be imposed by the king and it was seen that the day for Lutheranism in England had not yet dawned.

It will be sufficient here to quote the conclusion of Crumwell's letter, which dealt expressly with the matter in hand. " As for the Abbot of Reading and his monk," he writes, " if I find them as ye say they are, I will order them

as I think good.[1] Ye shall do well to do your
duty ; if you do so ye shall have no cause to
mistrust my friendship. If ye do not, I can
tell that (to) you, and that somewhat after the
plainest sort. To take a controversy out of
your hands into mine I do but mine office.
You meddle further than your office will bear
you, thus roughly to handle me for using of
mine. If ye do so no more I let pass all that
is past."

Whatever advantage the Abbot of Reading
derived temporarily, at different conjunctures,
from the king's partiality for him, it was by
this time clear that such favour could be continued to a man of Abbot Cook's character
only by the sacrifice of principles and convictions. According to the writer of the sermon
already quoted, the abbot "could not abide"
the preachers of the new-fangled doctrines then
in vogue, and "called them heretics and knaves
of the new learning." He was also "ever a

---

[1] Ultimately Roger London, the reader complained of by
Shaxton, found his way into the Tower. His name appears in
a list of prisoners there "on the 20th day of November," 1539,
as "Roger London, monk of Reading" (B. Mus. Cott. MS.,
Titus B. i., f. 133). His fate is uncertain.

great student and setter forth of St. Benet's, St. Francis', St. Dominic's and St. Augustine's rules, and said they were rules right holy and of great perfectness." It was, moreover, recognised that discipline was well maintained at Reading and Colchester no less than at Glastonbury; "these doughty deacons," as the writer calls the abbots and their monks, "thought it both heresy and treason to God to leave matins unsaid, to speak loud in the cloisters, and to eat eggs on the Friday."[1] It would appear probable that Abbot Cook did not refuse to take the oath of royal supremacy, although there can be little doubt that in so doing he did not intend to separate himself from the traditional teaching of the Catholic Church on the question of papal authority. "He thought to shoot at the king's supremacy," as the contemporary witness has put it, and he was apparently charged with saying "that he would pray for the pope's holiness as long as he lived and would once a week say mass for him, trusting that by such good

---

[1] R. O. State Papers, Domestic, 1539, 251.

prayers the pope should rise again and have the king's highness with all the whole realm in subjection as he hath had in time past. And upon a *bon voyage* would call him pope as long as he lived."

After a page of abuse, the writer continues: " I cannot tell how this prayer will be allowed among St. Benet's rules, but this I am certain and sure of, that it standeth flatly against our Master Christ's rule. . . . What other thing should the abbat pray for here (as me-thinketh) but even first and foremost for the high dishonouring of Almighty God, for the confusion of our most dread sovereign lord, king Henry VIII., with his royal successors, and also for the utter destruction of this most noble realm of England. Well, I say no more, but I pray God heartily that the mass be not abused in the like sort of a great many more in England which bear as fair faces under their black cowls and bald crowns as ever did the abbat of Reading, or any of the other traitors. I wiss neither the abbat of Reading, the abbat of Glassenbury, nor the prior [*sic*] of Colches-ter, Dr. Holyman, nor Roger London, John

Rugg, nor Bachelor Giles, blind Moore, nor Master Manchester, the warden of the friars ; no, nor yet John Oynyon, the abbat's chief councillor, was able to prove with all their sophistical arguments that the mass was ordained for any such intent or purpose as the abbat of Reading used it."

" I fear me, Hugh Cook was master cook to a great many of that black guard (I mean black monks), and taught them to dress such gross dishes as he was always wont to dress, that he is to say, treason ; but let them all take heed."

At the time of the great northern rising, the Abbey of Reading, together with those of Glastonbury and Colchester, is found on the list of contributors to the king's expenses in defeating the rebel forces. Reading itself appears to have had some communication with Robert Aske, for copies of a letter written by him, and apparently also his proclamation, were circulated in the town. Amongst others who were supposed to be privy to the intentions of the insurgent chief was John Eynon, a priest of the Church of St. Giles, Reading, and a special friend of Abbot Cook. Three years later this priest was executed with the abbot ; but it is clear that at the time there was not even a suggestion of any complicity in the insurrection on the part of the abbot, as he presided at the examinations held in December, 1536, as to this matter.[1]

The first sign of any serious trouble appears about the close of 1537. The king's proceedings, which were distasteful to the nation at large, naturally gave rise to much criticism and murmuring. Every overt expression of disapprobation was eagerly watched for and diligently inquired into by the royal officials. The numerous records of examinations as to words spoken in conversation or in sermons, evidence the extreme care taken by the government to crush out the first sparks of popular discontent. Rumours as to the king's bad health, or, still more, reports as to his death, were construed into indications of a treasonable disposition. In December, 1537, a rumour of this kind that Henry was dead reached Reading, and Abbot

---

[1] Calendar, xi., 1231.

Cook wrote to some of his neighbours to tell them what was reported. This act was laid to his charge, and Henry acquired a cheap reputation for magnanimity and clemency by pardoning "his own abbot" for what was, at the very worst, but a trifling act of indiscretion.

The libeller thus treats the incident :—"For think ye that the Abbat of Reading deserved any less than to be hanged, what time as he wrote letters of the king's death unto divers gentlemen in Berkshire, considering in what a queasy case the realm stood in at that same season? For the insurrection that was in the north country was scarcely yet thoroughly quieted; thus began he to stir the coals *à novo* and to make a fresh roasting fire, and did enough, if God had not stretched forth His helping hand, to set the realm in as great an uproar as ever it was, and yet the king's majesty, of his royal clemency, forgave him. This had been enough to have made this traitor a true man if there had been any grace in him."

Circumstances had brought Abbot Cook into communication with both the other abbots,

whose fate was subsequently linked with his
own.   In the triennial general chapters of the
Benedictines, in parliament, in convocation
they had frequently met ; and when the more
active measures of persecution devised by
Crumwell made personal intercourse impossible,
a trusty agent was found in the person of a
blind harper named Moore, whose affliction and
musical skill had brought him under the kindly
notice of the king.   This staunch friend of the
papal party, whose blindness rendered his
mission unsuspected, travelled about from one
abbey to another, encouraging the imprisoned
monks, bearing letters from house to house,
and, doubtless, finding a safe way of sending off
to Rome the letters which they had written to
the pope and cardinals.

   " But now amongst them all let us talk a
word or two of William Moor, the blind
harper.   Who would have thought that he
would have consented or concealed any treason against the king's majesty? or who
could have thought that he had had any
power thereto?   Who can muse or marvel
enough to see a blind man for lack of sight

to grope after treason? Oh! Moor, Moor, hast thou so great a delight and desire to play the traitor? Is this the mark that blind men trust to hit perchance? Hast thou not heard how the blind eateth many a fly? Couldst not thou beware and have kept thy mouth close together for fear of gnats? Hath God endued thee with the excellency of harping and with other good qualities, to put unto such a vile use? Couldst thou have passed the time with none other song but with the harping upon the string of treason? Couldst thou not have considered that the king's grace called thee from the wallet and the staff to the state of a gentleman? Wast thou also learned, and couldst thou not consider that the end of treason is eternal damnation? Couldst thou not be contented truly to serve thy sovereign lord king Henry VIII., whom thou before a great many oughtest and wast most bound truly to serve? Couldst not thou at least for all the benefits received at his grace's hand, bear towards him thy good will? Hadst thou nought else to do but to become a traitorous

messenger between abbat and abbat? Had
not the traitorous abbats picked out a pretty
mad messenger of such a blind buzzard as
thou art? Could I blazon thine arms sufficiently although I would say more than I have
said? Could a man paint thee out in thy
colours any otherwise than traitors ought to be
painted? Shall I call thee William Moor, the
blind harper? Nay, verily, thou shalt be called
William Moor, the blind traitor. Now, surely,
in my judgment, God did a gracious deed what
time He put out both thine eyes, for what a
traitor by all likelihood wouldst thou have been
if God had lent thee thy sight, seeing thou wast
so willing to grope blindfolded after treason!
When thou becamest a traitorous messenger
between the traitorous abbats, and when thou
tookest in hand to lead traitors in the trade of
treason, then was verified the sentence of our
Master Christ, which sayeth, When the blind
lead the blind both shall fall into the ditch.
Thou wast blind in thine eyes, and they were
blind in their consciences. Wherefore ye be
all fallen into the ditch, that is to say, into the
high displeasure of God and the king. I wiss,

Moor, thou wrestest thine harpstrings clean out of tune, and settest thine harp a note too high when thou thoughtest to set the bawdy bishop of Rome above the king's majesty."[1]

It is evident that in the Benedictine monasteries of the district as years went on there were many who, as they came to realise the true meaning of this new royal supremacy, made no attempt to dissemble their real opinions on the matter. The writer so frequently referred to thus expresses his conviction as to the attitude of the monks : " But like as of late by God's purveyance a great part of their religious hoods be already meetly well ripped from their crafty coats, even so I hope the residue of the like religion shall in like sort not long remain unripped ; for truly so long as they be let run at riot thus still in religion, they think verily that they may play the traitors

---

[1] State Papers, 1539, No. 251, p. 25. "William Moor" appears in a list of prisoners in the Tower, 20th November, 1539 (B. Mus. Cott. MS., Titus B. i., f. 133). Perhaps Moor is the same person mentioned by Stowe (ed. 1614, p. 582) : " The 1 of July (1540) a Welchman, a minstrel, was hanged and quartered for singing of songs which were interpreted to be prophecying against the king."

by authority. But now his grace seeth well enough that all was not gold that glittered, neither all his true subjects that called him lord and master, namely, of Balaam's asses with the bald crowns. But I would now heartily wish," he adds, writing after the execution of the Abbots of Glastonbury, Colchester and Reading, " that as many as be of that traitorous religion [*i.e.*, order] that those abbots were of, at the next [assizes] may have their bald crowns as well shaven as theirs were."

On such suspicions as these the Abbot of Abingdon was called up to London and examined by Crumwell himself, whilst one of his monks was removed from the abbey to Bishop Shaxton's prison, evidently for his opinions on religious questions of the day, since he is designated by the Bishop as "the popish monk." Again one of Crumwell's spies reported his grave doubts as to Sir Thomas Eliot. It appears that Eliot had given out that he had himself told Crumwell that "the Imperator of Almayn never spoke of the Bishop of Rome but he raised his bonnet," and that he consorted in the country with "the vain-glorious Abbot of Eynesham," and with Dr. Holyman, evidently a relative of Dom John Holyman, the monk of Reading, and incumbent of "Hanborough, a mile of Eynesham," who is noted as "a base priest and privy fautor of the Bishop of Rome." Moreover, "he was marvellous familiar," so said the spy, "with the Abbot of Reading and Doctor London, Warden of New College, Oxon," a man, it is to be observed, in every way of different mind from his namesake, Dr. London, the royal visitor.

A letter from Eliot to Crumwell, in which he expresses his willingness to give up his popish books and strives to remove from the mind of the all-powerful vicar-general of the king the suspicion that he was "an advancer of the pompous authority of the Bishop of Rome," gives some insight into the nature of his communications with the suspected abbots. There "hath happened," he says, "no little contention betwixt me and such persons as ye have thought that I especially favoured, even as ye also did,[1] for some laudable qualities which we

---

[1] The writer here evidently refers to the Abbot of Reading in particular.

10

supposed to be in them ; but neither they
could persuade me to approve that which both
my faith and reason condemned, nor I could
not dissuade them from the excusing of that

MONOGRAM OF ABBOT COOK, OR FARINGDON, FROM A
CONTEMPORARY PIECE OF STAINED GLASS.

which all the world abhorred. This obstinacy
of both parts relented the great affection betwixt us and withdrew our familiarity."[1]

In view of the prize to be won, that is, the

---

[1] Strype, *Ecclesiastical Memorials*, ii., ii., p. 229.

broad acres and other possessions of the great
monastic houses, any very definite enquiry as
to the opinions of the inmates was not at
once pressed home.   Crumwell played a waiting game.   The situation at Reading Abbey is
well described by Dr. London, the visitor and
royal agent in dissolving the religious houses,
in a letter written to Crumwell whilst occupied
in suppressing the Grey Friars' house in the
town.   " My lord," he writes of the abbot,
"doubteth my being here very sore, yet I
have not seen him since I came, nor been at
his house, except yesterday to hear mass.
The last time I was here he said, as they all
do, that he was at the king's command, but
loathe be they to come to any free surrender."[1]

Still Crumwell evidently hesitated to try conclusions, and so matters remained for another
year until he had obtained his Act of Parliament which provided for the case of a house
"happening to come to the king's highness by
attainder or attainders of treason."   By the
autumn of the year 1539 he was prepared for

---

[1] Gairdner, *Calendar*, xiii., ii., No. 5.

the final issue in the case of Reading. We have no records giving the details of Abbot Cook's arrest and his conveyance to the Tower. There is only the ominous entry in Crumwell's *Remembrances* early in September : " For proceeding against the abbots of Glaston, Reading and other in their countries." The Abbot of Reading seems to have been the first to be arrested, and there can be no doubt that they all remained for near two months in the Tower and were all subjected to the same enquiries. There is evidence to show that at Reading many arrests were made when the abbot was taken. A list of the prisoners in Tower on November 20th, 1539, includes the following, all connected with the abbey and town : Roger London, monk of Reading, Peter Lawrence, Warden of the Grey Friars at Reading, Giles Coventry, who was a friar of the same house, George Constantine, Richard Manchester and William Moor, " the blind harper ; "[1] and in one of Crumwell's *Remembrances* at this time there is noted : " Item to proceed

---

[1] B. Mus., Cott. M.S., Titus, B. i., f. 133.

against the Abbots of Reading, Glaston,
Rugg, Bachyler, London, the Grey Friars
and Heron."

Abbot Cook, like the Abbot of Glastonbury,
underwent examination and practical condemnation in the Tower before being sent down to
his "country to be tried and executed." What
was the head and chief of his offence we may
take from the testimony of the hostile witness
so freely used.

"It will make many beware to put their
fingers in the fire any more," he says, "either
for the honour of Peter and Paul or for the
right of the Roman Church. No, not for the
pardon of the pope himself, though he would
grant more pardon than all the popes that
ever were have granted. I think, verily, our
mother holy Church of Rome hath not so
great a jewel of her own darling Reynold Poole
as she should have had of these abbats if they
could have conveyed all things cleanly. Could
not our English abbats be contented with English forked caps but must look after Romish
cardinal hats also? Could they not be contented with the plain fashion of England but

FACSIMILE OF ABBOT COOK'S WRITING, FROM A LETTER IN THE RECORD OFFICE ("AT REDYNG" THE 26 DAY OF JANUARY, BYYOUR DAYLY BEDEMAN, HUGH ABBAT THERE").

must counterfeit · the crafty cardinality of Reynold Poole? Surely they should have worn their cardinal hats with as much shame as that papistical traitor, Reynold Poole. . . Could not our popish abbats beware of Reynold Poole, of that bottomless whirlpool, I say, which is never satiate of treason?"

Carried down to Reading for the mockery of justice, called a trial, the abbot and his companions could not swerve from their belief and their faith, but they maintained that this was not treason against the king. "When these traitors" says the libeller, "were arraigned at the bar, although they had confessed before and written it with their own hands that they had committed high treason against the king's majesty, yet they found all the means they could to go about to try themselves true men, which was impossible to bring to pass."

The writer's object was not to state the facts, but to cover the memory of the dead men with obliquy. Taking the document, however, as a whole, and bearing in mind the interpretation placed on the word treason at that time, there is no difficulty in penetrating into his meaning.

On November 15th, the same day upon
which Abbot Whiting suffered at Glastonbury,
the Abbot of Reading and two priests, John
Eynon and John Rugg, were brought out to
suffer the death of traitors.   Here the same
ghastly scene was enacted as at Glastonbury ;
the stretching on the hurdle, the dragging
through the streets of the town.   Abbot Cook,
standing in the space before the gateway of
his abbey, spoke to the people who in great
numbers had gathered to witness the strange
spectacle of the execution of a lord abbot of the
great and powerful monastery of Reading.   He
told them of the cause for which he and his
companions were to die, not fearing openly to
profess that which Henry's laws made it treason to hold—fidelity to the see of Rome, which
he went on to point out was but the common
faith of those who had the best right to declare the true teaching of the English Church.
"The Abbot of Reading, at the day of his
death lamenting the miserable end that he
was come unto," says our authority, pervert-
ing words and deeds to the greater glory of
the king, "confessed before a great sight of

READING ABBEY GATEWAY.

Face p. 152.

people, and said that he might thank these
four privy traitors before named of his sore
fall, as who should say that those three bishops
and the vicar of Croydon had committed no
less treason than he had done. Now, good
Lord for his Passion, who would have thought
that these four holy men would have wrought
in their lifetime such detestable treason?" And
later on, speaking of the three abbots: "God
caused, I say, not only their treason to be
disclosed and come abroad in such a wonderful sort as never was heard of, which were
too long to recite at this time, but also dead.
men's treason that long lay hidden under the
ground; that is to say, the treason of the
old bishop of Canterbury [Warham], the treason of the old bishop of St. Asaph [Stan-
dish], the treason of the old vicar of Croydon,
and the treason of the old bishop of London
[Stokesley], which four traitors had concealed
as much treason by their lives' time as any of
these traitors that were put to death.[1]   There

---

[1] This reference to Warham, Stokesley, &c., shows that what
was in question throughout the proceedings was the papal
versus the royal authority.

was never a barrel better herring to choose
[among] them all, as it right well appeared by
the Abbat of Reading's confession made at the
day of [execution], who I daresay accused none
of them for malice nor hatred.   For the abbat
as heartily loved those holy fathers as ever he
loved any men in his life."

Thus, from the scaffold with the rope round
his neck, and on the verge of eternity, the
venerable abbot gave a witness to the veneration traditional in these islands from the
earliest ages for the see of Rome, "in which
the Apostles daily sit, and their blood shows
forth without intermission the glory of God."[1]

When the abbot had finished, John Eynon,[2]
the abbot's "chief counsellor," also spoke,
evidently in the same sense, and begged the
prayers of the bystanders for his soul, and

---

[1] In these terms the first council of Arles, in 314, address
Pope St. Silvester.   This is the first known official act proceeding from bishops of the British Church.

[2] The usual spelling of this name has been Onyon or Oynyon,
but it really was Eynon.   It is so spelt in the document already
referred to (*Calendar*, xi., No. 1231), and also in the accurate
entry of the conviction, to be found on the Controlment Roll,
31 Hen. VIII., m. 28 d.   "Recordum attinctionis, &c., Hugonis
abbatis monasterii de Redyng in dict. com. Berks. alias dicti

the king's forgiveness if in aught he had offended.[1]

This over, the sentence of hanging with its barbarous accessories was carried out upon

---

Hugonis Cooke, nuper de Redyng in eodem com. Berks. clerici ; Johannis Eynon nuper de Redyng in com. pred. clerici ; Johannis Rugge nuper de Redyng in com. Berks. clerici alias dict. Johannis Rugge nuper de Redyng capellani pro quibusdam altis proditionibus unde eorum quilibet pro se indictus fuit, tractus et suspensus."

[1] It would seem that at the trial some attempt was made to implicate Eynon in the Pilgrimage of Grace, in connection with which his name had been mentioned in 1536 ; and this is doubtless the "treason" which the hostile witness declares that he not only denied, " but also stoutly and stubbornly withstood it even to the utmost, evermore finding great fault with justice, and oftentimes casting his arms abroad, said : 'Alas, is this justice to destroy a man guiltless ? I take it between God and my soul that I am as clear in this matter as the child that was this night born.' Thus he prated and made a work as though he had not known what the matter had meant, thinking to have faced it out with a card of ten. And in this sort he held on even from the time of the arraignment till he came to the gallows. Marry then, when he saw none other way but one, his heart began somewhat to relent. Then both he and his companions, with their ropes about their necks confessed before all the people that were present that they had committed high treason against the king's most noble person, but namely Oynyon, for he said that he had offended the king's grace in such sort of treason that it was not expedient to tell thereof. Wherefore he besought the people not only to pray unto God for him, but also desired them, or some of them at the least, to desire the king's grace of his merciful goodness to forgive it his soul, for else he was sure, as he said, to be damned.

Abbot·Cook and the two priests, John Eynon and John Rugg.[1]

The attainder of the abbot, according to the royal interpretation of the law, placed the Abbey of Reading and its lands and possessions at Henry's disposal. In fact, as in the case of Glastonbury, on the removal of the abbot to the Tower in September, 1539, before either trial or condemnation, the pillage of the abbey had been commenced. As early as September 8th Thomas Moyle wrote from Reading that he, "master Vachell and Mr.

_____

And yet not an hour before a man that had heard him speak would have thought verily that he had been guiltless of treason."

[1] Eynon was, as before stated, a priest attached to the church of St. Giles, Reading. John Rugg had formerly held a prebend at Chichester, but had apparently retired to Reading. In December, 1531 (*Calendar*, v.), Rugg writes for his books to be sent to Reading from Chichester. Another letter, dated Feb. 3, 1532, from "your abbey-lover Jo. Rugg" shows that the writer had obtained dispensation for non-residence at Chichester. Coates (*Reading*, p. 261), on the authority of Croke, says that John Rugg was indicted for saying "the king's highness cannot be Supreme Head of the Church of England." On being asked "What did you for saving your conscience when you were sworn to take the king for Supreme Head?" Rugg replied, "I added this condition in my mind, to take him for Supreme Head in temporal things, but not in spiritual things."

READING ABBEY RUINS.

Face p. 157.

Dean of York" (Layton) had "been through
the inventory of the plate, etc., at the resi-
dence" there. "In the house," he said, "there
is a chamber hanged with three pieces of metely
good tapestry. It will serve well for hanging
a mean little chamber in the king's majesty's
house." This is all they think worth keeping
for the royal use. "There is also," the writer
adds, "a chamber hung with six pieces of
verdure with fountains, but it is old and at the
ends of some of them very foul and greasy."
He notes several beds with silk hangings, and
in the church eight pieces of tapestry, "very
goodly" but small, and concludes by saying
that he and his fellows think that the sum of
£200 a year "will serve for pensions for the
monks."[1]

On September 15th another commissioner,
Richard Pollard, wrote from Reading that he
had dispatched certain goods according to
Crumwell's direction "and part of the stuff

---

[1] R. O. *Crumwell Correspondence*, xxix., No. 76. In the
"Corporation diary," quoted in Coates' *Reading*, p. 261, is the
entry "before which said nineteenth of September (1539), the
monastery is suppressed and the abbot is deprived, and after
this suppression all things remain in the king's hands"

reserved for the king's majesty's use."   " The
whole house and church are," he says, "still
undefaced," and "as for the plate,[1] vestments,
copes and hangings, which we have reserved"
to the king's use, they are left in good custody
and are to be at once conveyed to London.
" Thanks be to God," he adds, "everything is
well finished, and every man well contented,
and   giveth   humble   thanks   to   the   king's
grace."[2]

---

[1] In Pollard's account of the plate of "attainted persons and
places " (*Monastic Treasures, Abbotsford Club*, p. 38) Reading
is credited with 19½ ozs. of gold, 377 ozs. of gilt plate, and 2,660
ozs. of silver. It is also stated that the abbot put "to gage to
Sir W. Luke three gilt bowls of 152 ozs. and six silver bowls of
246 ozs."

[2] Wright, 220. Mr. Wright thinks this letter " must refer to
the priory and not to the abbey." A letter from William
Penison, to whom Pollard says he committed the charge "by
indenture," says that on September 11th he "received possession of the Abbey of Reading and all the domains which the
late abbot had in his hands at his late going away" (R. O.
Crumwell Correspondence, vol. xxxii., No. 36.) This letter
shows that to William Penison Abbot Cook was *late* abbot—
in other words, had ceased to hold the office when he was
taken away to the Tower for examination early in September.

CHAPTER IX.

THE LAST ABBOT OF COLCHESTER.

THE Abbot of St. John's, Colchester, Thomas Marshall,[1] writes Browne Willis, "was one of the three mitred parliamentary abbots that had courage enough to maintain his conscience and run the last extremity, being neither to be prevailed upon by bribery, terror or any dishonourable motives to come into a surrender, or subscribe to the king's supremacy; on which account, being attainted of high treason, he suffered death."

[1] Thomas Marshall was also called Beche. It may be worth while here, as some confusion has existed as to the last Abbot of Colchester, to give the evidence of the Controlment Roll, 31 Hen. VIII., m. 36d., which leaves no room for doubt that Beche and Marshall are *aliases* for the same person. "Recordum attinctionis Thomæ Beche nuper de West Donylands, in com. Essex, clerici, alias dicti Thomæ Marshall nuper de eisdem

Thomas Marshall succeeded Abbot Barton in June, 1533, and entered upon the cares of office at a time when religious life was becoming almost impossible. At the outset he had apparently considerable difficulty in obtaining possession of the temporalities of his abbey. " I, with the whole consent of my brethren," he writes to Crumwell, "have sealed four several obligations for the payment of £200 to the king's use, trusting now by your especial favour to have restitution of my temporalities with all other things pertaining to the same. Unless I have your especial favour and aid in recovering such rents and dues as are withdrawn from the monastery of late, and I not able to recover them by the law, I cannot tell how I shall live in the world, saving my truth and promises."[1]

villa et comit., clerici, alias Thomæ Beche nuper abbatis nuper monasterii S. Johannis Bapt. juxta Colcestr., in com. pred. jam dissolut. alias dicti Thomæ Marshall nuper abb. nuper mon. S. Johis. Colcestr. in com. pred. pro quibusdam aliis proditionibus." West Donylands was a manor belonging to the abbot, and the name occurs in exchanges made by the abbot with Chancellor Audley in 1536 (see *Calendar*, xi., Nos. 385, 519).

[1] R. O. *Crumwell Correspondence*, vi., f. 145. The temporalities were restored on Jan. 23rd, 1534, and on March 30th of this

Of the earlier career of Thomas Marshall
little is known except that he, like the majority
of his order in England who were selected by
their superiors for a university course, was sent
to Oxford, where he resided for several years,
and passed through the schools with credit to
himself and his order.   During this period he
was probably an inmate of St. Benedict's or
Gloucester Hall, the largest of the three estab-
lishments which the Benedictines possessed
in Oxford, and to which the younger religious
of most of the English abbeys were sent to
pursue their higher studies.[1]

Very shortly after Abbot Marshall's election

---

same year the new abbot took his seat in the House of Lords.   It
has been thought that Marshall is the same Thomas Marshall
who ruled the abbey of Chester until 1530, and is counted as the
twenty-sixth abbot of that house (*Monasticon*, iv.).   Whether,
on his retirement from Chester in favour of the reinstated
abbot, John Birchenshaw, he went to Colchester is uncertain.
If he had been long at this latter monastery it is somewhat
strange that the witnesses against him in 1539 should have
professed to be unacquainted with him until his election.

[1] St. Benedict's is now represented by Worcester College ;
Canterbury Hall, destined for the monks of the metropolitan
church, is now merged in Christ Church ; and Trinity College
has succeeded to St. Cuthbert's Hall, the learned home of the
monks of Durham.   D. Thomas Marshall, O.S.B., supplicated

11

his troubles commenced.   At Colchester, as
elsewhere in the country at this period, there
were to be found some only too anxious to win
favour to themselves by carrying reports of the
doings and sayings of their brethren to Crumwell or the king.   In April, 1534, a monk of
St. John's complained of the "slanderous and
presumptuous" sayings of the sub-prior, " D.
John Francis."   This latter monk, according
to Crumwell's informer, had "declared our
sovereign lord the king and his most honourable council, on the occasion of a new book of
articles, to be all heretics, whereas before he
said they were but schismatics."[1]   These and
other remarks were quite sufficient to have
brought both the bold monk himself and his
abbot into trouble at a time when the gossip
of the fratry or shaving-house was picked up by
eavesdroppers and carried to court to regale the
ears of the Lord Privy Seal.   In this case, however, the report came on the eve of the admini-

---

for B.D. January 24, 150? ; disputed 3rd June, 1511 ; admitted
to oppose 19th Oct. ; received the degree of S.T.B. 10th Dec. ;
sued for D.D. and disputed 20th April, 1515.   Boase, *Register
of the University of Oxford*, p. 63.

[1] *Calendar* 1534, Ap. viii.

stration to the monks of Colchester of what
was to be henceforth considered the touchstone
of loyalty, the oath of supremacy.   On the 7th
of July, 1534, the oath was offered to the monks
in the chapter house of St. John's, and taken
by Abbot Marshall and sixteen monks, in-
cluding Dom John Francis, the subprior complained of to Crumwell.

   Very little indeed is known about Colchester or the doings of the abbot from this
time till his arrest in 1539.   At the time
of the northern rising, whilst the commissioners for gaol-delivery sat at Colchester,
they were invited to dine at the abbey with
the Abbot of St. John's.   When they were
at dinner, as Crumwell's informant writes to
him, one Marmaduke Nevill and others came
into the hall.   " I asked him," says the
writer, ' How do the traitors in the north ? '
' No traitors, for if ye call us traitors we
will call you heretics.' "   Nevill then went
on to say that the king had pardoned them,
or they had not been at Colchester.   They
were, he declared, 30,000 well-horsed, and " I
am sure," he said, " my lord abbot will make

me good cheer;" and asked why, said,
"Marry, for all the abbeys in England be
beholden to us, for we have set up all the
abbeys again in our country, and though it
were never so late they sang mattins the same
night." He added that in the north they were
"plain fellows," and southern men, though they
"thought as much, durst not utter it."[1]

Another glimpse of the life led by the Abbot
of Colchester during the few troubled years
of his authority is afforded by a writer of a
slightly subsequent period :—

"Those who can call to mind the cruel
deeds of Henry VIII., the confusion of things
sacred and profane, and the slaughterings of
which he was the author, will have no difficulty
in recollecting the case of John Beche, Abbat
of Colchester. Excelling many of the abbats
of his day in devotion, piety and learning, the
sad fate of the cardinal (Fisher) and the execution of Sir Thomas More oppressed him with
grief and bitterness. For he had greatly
loved them ; and as he had honoured them

---

[1] *Calendar*, xi., 1319.

when living, so now that they had so gladly
suffered death for the Church's unity, he began
to reverence and venerate them, and often and
much did he utter to that effect, and made his
friends partakers of his grief which the late
events had caused him.   And he was in the
habit of extolling the piety, meekness, and
innocence of the late martyrs to those guests
whom he invited to his table, and who came to
him of their own will, some of whom assented
to his words, while others listened in silence.
There came at length a traitorous guest, a
violator of the sacred rights of hospitality,
who by his words incited the abbat to talk
about the execution of the cardinal and More,
hoping to entrap him in his speech.   Thereon
the abbat, who could not be silent on such a
theme spoke indeed in their praise but with
moderation and sparingly, adding at last that
he marvelled what cause of complaint the king
could have found in men so virtuous and
learned, and the greatest ornaments of Church
and State, as to deem them unworthy of longer
life, and to condemn them to a most cruel
death.   These words did this false friend carry

away in his traitorous breast, to make them
known in due season to the advisers of the
king. What need of more? The abbat is
led to the same tribunal which had condemned
both Fisher and More, and there received the
like sentence of death; yea, his punishment
was the more cruel than theirs, for in his case
no part of the sentence was remitted. Thus
he was added as the third to the company of
the two former. But why should I call him
the third, and try to enumerate the English
martyrs of that time, who are past counting?
The writers of our annals mention many by
name, but there were many more whose names
they could not ascertain, whose number is
known to God alone, for whose cause they
died. Yet I hope that some day God will
make known their names and the resting-places
of their bodies, which were in life the dwelling-
places of His Holy Spirit."[1]

About the time of the arrest of the Abbots of
Reading and Glastonbury, in September, 1539,
reports were spread as to the approaching dis-

---

[1] B. Mus. Arundel MS., 152, f. 235 d.

The Gateway of Colchester Abbey.

solution of St. John's, Colchester. Sir Thomas
Audley, the chancellor, endeavoured to avert
what he thought would be an evil thing for the
county. He had heard the rumours about the
destruction of the two abbeys of St. John's,
Colchester, and St. Osyth's, and, writing to
Crumwell, he begs they may continue, " not, as
they be, religious ; but that the king's majesty
of his goodness to translate them into colleges.
For the which, as I said to you before, his
grace may have of either of them £1,000,
that is for both £2,000, and the gift of the
deans and prebendaries at his own pleasure.
The cause I move this is, first, I consider that
St. John's standeth in his grace's own town at
Colchester, wherein dwell many poor people
who have daily relief of the house. Another
cause, both these houses be in the end of the
shire of Essex, where little hospitality will be
kept if these be dissolved. For as for St.
John's it lacketh water, and Saint Osyth's
standeth in the marshes, not very wholesome,
so that few of reputation, as I think, will keep
continual houses in any of them unless it be a
congregation as there is now. There are also

twenty houses, great and small, dissolved in
the shire of Essex already." Audley then goes
on to protest that he only asks for the common
good, and can get no advantage himself by the
houses being allowed to continue, and concludes by offering Crumwell £200 for himself
if he can persuade the king to grant his request.[1]

The circumstances attending Abbot Marshall's arrest are unknown, but by the begin-
ing of November, 1539, he was certainly in the
Tower.   On the 1st of that month Edmund
Crowman, who had been his servant ever since
he had been abbot, was under examination.
All that was apparently extracted from this
witness was that a year before the abbot had
given him certain plate to take care of and
" £40 in a coser."[2]

The abbot's chaplain was also interrogated as
to any words he had heard the abbot speak
against the king at any time, but little information was elicited from him.   The most impor-

---

[1] Wright, p. 246.
[2] R. O. *Crumwell Correspondence*, xxxviii., No. 42.

tant piece of evidence is a document, which, as it contains declarations as to Abbot Marshall's opinions upon several important matters, and as it is almost the only record of the examinations of witnesses against any of the three abbots, and gives a sample of the questions on which all these examinations in the Tower concerning treason must have turned, may here be given as nearly as possible in the original form.

Interrogatories ministered unto Robert Rowse, mercer, of Colchester, 4to Novembris anno regni Henrici octavi tricesimo primo (1539). Ad primam, the said Rowse sworne upon the Evangel, and sayeth that he hath known the Abbat of Colchester the space of six years at midsummer last past or thereabout, about which time the said —— was elected abbat.[1] And within a sennight after or thereabout this examinant sent unto the said abbat a dish of bass (baces) and a pottle of wine to the welcome. Upon the which present the said abbat did send for the examinant to dine with him upon a Friday, at which time they were first acquainted, and since was divers times in his company and familiar with him unto a fortnight before the feast of All Hallows was two years past.—ROBERT ROWSE.

2. Ad secundam, he sayeth that the principal cause why that he did leave the company of the said abbat was because that abbat was divers times communing

---

[1] D. Thomas Marshall or Beche was elected June 10th, 1533.

and respuing against the king's majesty's   *Supremacy.*
supremacy and such ordinances as were passed by the
act of Parliament concerning the extinguishment of the
bishop of Rome's usurped authority, saying that the
whole authority was given by Christ unto   *The whole*
Peter and to his successors, bishops of   *authority*
Rome, to bind and to loose, and to grant   *committed to Peter.*
pardons for sin, and to be chief and supreme head of
the Church throughout all Christian realms immediate
and next unto Christ, and that it was against God's
commandment and His laws that any   *Against the*
temporal prince should be head of the   *supremacy.*
Church. And also he said that the king's highness had
evil counsel that moved him to take on hand to be chief
head of the Church of England and to pull down these
houses of religion which were founded by his grace's
progenitors and many noble men for the service and
honour of God, the commonwealth, and relief of poor
folk, and that the same was both against   *Against man's*
God's law and man's law; and further-   *law and God's*
more, he said that by means of the pre-   *law.*
mises the king and his council were drawn into such an
inordinate covetousness that if all the water in the
Thames were flowing gold and silver it   *Covetous.*
were not able to slake their covetousness, and said a
vengeance of all such councillors. —   *A vengeance.*
ROBERT ROWSE.

3. Ad tertiam, he sayeth that he is not well remembered of the year nor of the days that the said abbat had
the foresaid communications because he spoke at divers
times, and specially at such times as he heard that any
such matters were had in use, and furthermore of this
he is well remembered of that at such time as the monks

of Syon, the Bishop of Rochester, and Sir Thomas More were put to execution, the said abbat would say that he marvelled greatly of such tyranny as was   Tyranny. used by the king and his council to put such holy men to death, and further the abbat said that in his opinion they died holy martyrs and in the right of   Died martyrs. Christ's Church.—ROBERT ROWSE.

4. Ad quartam, he sayeth that the last time that ever he heard the said abbat have any communication of such matters was, immediately after that he heard of the insurrection in the north parts, he sent for this examinant to come to sup with him, and in the mean time that supper was making ready the abbat and the examinant were walking between the hall and the garden in a little gallery off the ground, and then and there the abbat asked of this examinant what news he heard of the coast? and this examinant said that he heard none.   Then the abbat said : " Dost you not hear of the insurrection in the north?" and   Northern this examinant said "no."   "The north-   men. ern lads be up and they begin to take pip in the webe (*sic*) and say plainly that they will have no more abbeys suppressed in their country ;" and he said to this examinant that the northern men were as true subjects unto the king as anywhere within his realm, and that they desired nothing of the king but that they might have delivered unto their hands the Archbishop of Canterbury, the lord chancellor, and the   That these lord privy seal ; and the abbat said " would   lords might to God that the northern men had them,   be delivered to the northern for then (he said) we should have a merry   men. world, for they were three arch-heretics,"   Arch-heretics, which term this examinant never heard before ; and so

then they went to supper, and since this time, which was as this examinant doth remember a fortnight or three weeks before the feast of All Saints, was two years.— ROBERT ROWSE.[1]

The evidence of Thomas Nuthake, a "physition," of Colchester, is to the like effect. He had not, he said, to his knowledge seen or known Abbot Thomas before his election, although he had divers times repaired to the abbey before that time. In reply to the third question, this doctor "sayeth that concerning the marriage of queen Anne this examinant remembers he hath heard the said abbat say that the reason why the king's highness did forsake the bishop of Rome was to the intent that his majesty might be divorced from the lady dowager and wed queen Anne, and therefore his grace refused to take the bishop of Rome for the supreme head of the Church, and made himself the supreme head."[1]

Another of the witnesses against the Lord Abbot of Colchester was a cleric, John Seyn,

---

[1] R. O. State Papers, Dom., 1539, $\frac{v}{20.r}$. The marginal notes copied from the original document, indicate the chief points on which the examination turned.

[1] *Ibid.*, $\frac{v}{206}$.

ABBOT BECHE'S PECTORAL CROSS.

Face p. 173.

who deposed that when he had informed him
of his neighbour, the Abbot of St. Osyth's surrender of his monastery to the king, he answered, " I will not say the king shall never
have *my* house, but it will be against my will
and against my heart, for I know by my
learning that he cannot take it by right and
law, wherefore in my conscience I cannot be
content, nor he shall never have it with my
heart and will." Whereunto John Seyn, clerk,
answered in this wise : " Beware of such learning as ye learned at Oxenford when ye were
young. Ye would be hanged and ye are
worthy. I will advise you to conform yourself as a true subject, or else you shall hinder
your brethren and also yourself."[1]

Nothing more is known of Abbot Marshall's
last days, but the fact of his execution as a
traitor on December 1st, 1539. The enamelled
pectoral cross of the venerable martyr has been
preserved, and is now in possession of the Lord
Clifford of Chudleigh. On one side it bears the
emblems of the Five Wounds, in the centre the

---

[1] R. O. *Cromwell Correspondence*, xxxviii., No. 41

Sacred Heart of our Lord, surrounded by the
crown of thorns, above which is the inscription,
" I.N.R.I.," and below it the sacred monogram,
" I.H.S." with the wounded hands and feet of
our Saviour.   On the back the instruments
of the Passion are engraved.   The following
inscriptions in Latin appear in and about the
cross : "May the Passion of our Lord Jesus
Christ bring us out of sorrow and sadness.
This sign of the cross shall be in the heavens
when our Lord shall come to judgment.   Be-
hold, O man! thy Redeemer suffers for thee.
He who will come after me, let him take up his
cross and follow me."

It is curious to observe how frequently in
this world malice defeats its own ends even
when it takes a guise, to some persons apparently so attractive, of doing God a service.   It
is by a singular fate that the would-be preacher,
who gave himself so much trouble to defame
the three Abbots of Glastonbury, Reading and
Colchester and their companions, in the expec-

CASE OF ABBOT BECHE'S PECTORAL CROSS.

Face p. 174.

tation doubtless of thereby recommending himself to the king, should have been, after three
centuries and a half of oblivion, the most explicit witness of the cause for which these
venerable men gave up their lives in all the
terrors of as shameful and painful a death as
man could devise.

The writer himself amid the periods which
betoken his unhappy spirit, seems to have been
haunted still with some forebodings that he
was destined to make manifest a truth which it
was the evident design of those in power to
shroud in obscurity. He cannot help being
truculent even at his best; but the form which
he adopts may well be pardoned for the sake
of the sense. " Is it not to be thought, trow
ye," he says, "that forasmuch as these trusty
traitors have so valiantly jeopardied a joint for
the Bishop of Rome's sake, that his Holiness
will after their hanging canvass them, canonise
them, I would say, for their labours and pains.
It is not to be doubted but his Holiness will
look upon their pains as upon Thomas Becket's,
seeing it is for like matter."

Much has since happened which the writer

of these words could not have anticipated.   In
God's hands are times and seasons, and He
alone it is Who judges rightly the acts and lives
of men.   The words of the wise man fittingly
rise up in the mind as it recalls the story of the
deaths of these holy abbots.   " In the sight of
the unwise they seemed to die : and their de-
parture was taken for misery, and their going
away from us for utter destruction : but they
are in peace.   And though in the sight of men
they suffered torments, their hope is full of
immortality.   Afflicted in few things, in many
they shall be well rewarded ; because God has
tried them and found them worthy of Himself.
As gold in the furnace He hath proved them,
and as a victim of a holocaust He hath received
them, and in time there shall be respect had
unto them."

APPENDIX I.

In view of the want of information as to the internal arrangement of the monasteries on the eve of their suppression, caused by the wholesale destruction of documents, and especially as regards the music and church services, the following paper printed in the *Reliquary* (*New Series*, vol. vi., p. 176) seems of sufficient interest to be given here.

From the document it may be gathered that at Glastonbury there were always three organists: a chief organist and master of the singing boys, appointed for life; and two youths, who in consideration of a musical education, were bound (after two years' instruction) to serve as assistant organists for six years. It must be understood that the chief duties of these organists and of the singing boys were confined to the masses and offices chaunted in the chapel of the Blessed Virgin. These were, of course, not monastic, that is to say, they were outside of the ordinary conventual life, and were not followed necessarily by the monks. These services were evidently carried out with every accessory calculated to call forth popular devotion to the Blessed Virgin, and there can be little doubt that the sweet strains of melody heard every day in this special sanctuary of the Mother of God attracted thither high and low, rich and poor, who might find as an ordinary rule

12

but little to call them to the more formal and simple offices daily said by the monks themselves in the high choir.

It is this music in the chapels of Our Blessed Lady in monasteries *apud Brittannos*, which calls forth the censures of that occasionally severe and always erratic moralist Erasmus (*Annot. ad* 1 Cor. xiv. 26).

We have no means of saying whether on festival days the monks of Glastonbury themselves used "that depraved kind of chaunt called *faubourdon*," though few persons at the present day will be inclined to see in the use of what is called "harmonised gregorians" any great enormity. It is, however, certain that on feasts and festal days the monastic offices in the "High Choir" of Glastonbury were accompanied with such beauty of music as the presence of the singing-school and the playing upon the organs, under the care of the chief organist, could give. For the rest the document will repay a careful perusal, and for those who are interested in the subject of ecclesiastical music in England at a time when it was assiduously cultivated, the indications and suggestions which it gives will be found to possess a high degree of interest. The spelling of the document has been modernised.

"This indenture made the tenth day of August, the 26th year of the reign of our Sovereign Lord King Henry VIII. (*i.e.*, 1534), between the Right Reverend Father in God, Richard Whiting, Abbot of the Monastery of Our Blessed Lady of Glastonbury and the Convent of the same, in the county of Somerset, of the one part, and James Renynger of Glastonbury foresaid, in the said county, Singingman, of the other part, witnesseth that the said James Renynger hath covenanted and granted and agreed, and by these presents

covenants, grants, and agrees to serve the said Reverend
Father and Convent, and their successors in the Monastery of Glastonbury foresaid, in his faculty of singing
and playing upon the organs (for the) term of his life
as well in (the) daily services of Our Lady kept in the
chapel of Our Blessed Lady in Glastonbury foresaid,
as daily mattins, masses, evensongs, compline, anthems
and all other divine services as hath been accustomably
used to be sung in the said chapel of Our Blessed Lady
of Glastonbury before the time of these covenants. And
to do service in singing and playing upon the organs in
the high choir of Glastonbury foresaid on all and all
manner such feasts and festival days as hath been in
times past used and accustomed there.

" And in likewise to serve the said Reverend Father
and his successors with songs and playing on instruments
of music as in the times of Christmas and other seasons,
as hath been heretofore used and accustomed and at any
other time or times when the said James Renynger
shall be thereunto required by the said Reverend
Father, his successor or assigns. And further the said
James Renynger covenants, grants and agrees to instruct and teach six children always at the pleasure
of the said Reverend Father or his successors for the
chapel of Our Blessed Lady in Glastonbury, sufficiently,
lawfully and melodiously with all his diligence in prick-
song and descant; of the which six children, two of
them yearly to be sufficiently instructed and taught by
the said James Renynger in playing on the organs for
the space of two years ; the said children to be always
chosen at the pleasure of the said Reverend Father and
his successors which he or they shall think to be most
apt thereto, so that the friends of the two children will
be bound in sufficient bonds that the said two children

and any of them shall serve the said Reverend Father
and his successors in singing and playing on the organs
daily in the said chapel of Our Lady and high choir of
the Monastery of Glastonbury aforesaid, and other
times of the year in manner and form as before rehearsed, for the space of six years next ensuing the said
two years of their teaching in singing and playing.
And the said Reverend Father and his successors shall
find the said James Renynger clavicords to teach the
said two children to play upon, for the which service well
and truly done the said Reverend Father and Convent
covenants and grants to the said James Renynger during his life as well in sickness as in health ten pounds
of lawful money of England, as well for his stipend as for
his meat and drink, at four principal times of the year in
equal portions at the Right Reverend Father's chequer
of receipt in Glastonbury to be taken and received,
and also once in every year his livery gown or else thirteen shillings and fourpence in money for the said gown,
always at the pleasure and election of the said Reverend
Father and his successors: also two loads of wood
brought home to the said James Renynger's house or
chamber (and his house rent free, or else thirteen
shillings and fourpence a year for it). Always (suppos-
ing) that if it happen the said James Renynger be taken
up by virtue of any of the King's commissions, or by
any authority of his, to serve his grace, that if the same
James Renynger come to Glastonbury again within one
year and one day the next following, and so from thence-
forth do his diligent service in singing and playing on
the organs, and teaching children at all times and in
everything accordingly in manner and form as is before
rehearsed, that then he should have his perpetuity again
without any interruption or let ; and also if it happen

the said James Renynger does not do his diligence in teaching and instructing the said six children in singing and playing, as is before rehearsed, to the pleasure of the said Reverend Father or his successors, or else if it happen that the said James be sick or aged so that he cannot well and diligently instruct and teach the said children, then it shall be lawful to the said Reverend Father and his successors as Abbots, of the said ten pounds (to deduct) for the teaching and instructing of the said six children yearly 105s. 4d.

"In witness whereof to the one part of these present indentures remaining with the said James Renynger, the aforesaid Reverend Father, Richard Whityng, Abbot of the foresaid Monastery of Glastonbury, and Convent of the same have put their convent seal and to the other part, remaining with the said foresaid Reverend Father and Convent, the foresaid James Renynger has put his seal.

"Given at Glastonbury aforesaid the day above said."

APPENDIX II.

THE following is a translation of an old paper kept with the pectoral cross of the last Abbot of Colchester. " This gold and enamelled cross belonged to Abbot John Beche, last superior of the Benedictine Abbey of St. John's, Colchester, in the county of Suffolk in England. He was elected Abbot in 1523, and refused, at the same time as the Abbots of Glastonbury and Reading, the act by which Henry VIII., King of England, was declared head of the Church, or to resign to his Majesty the property of his abbey. For this reason he was convicted of treason, and hanged in the said town of Colchester on December 1, 1539.

" This cross was preserved in the Mannock family, whose seat was in the neighbourhood of Colchester, up to the time of the last baronet, Sir George Mannock, who gave it to the English Benedictine nuns then at Brussels, and since settled in Winchester, where two of his sisters were nuns. About the year 1788, the cross was given by the abbess of that community to the late Mr. Weld, whose aunt had long lived among them."

In this account there are certain inaccuracies which, however, do not affect the truth of the tradition as to the cross. The Mannocks' family seat was Gifford Hall, not far from Colchester and in the county of Suffolk. The Mannocks never lost the Catholic faith,

and at least four members of the family were professed
among the English Benedictine nuns of Brussels in
the last century. One of these, Dame Etheldreda
Mannock, was Abbess from 1762 to 1773. Three of
the nuns were sisters to Sir George Mannock, who
presented Abbot Beche's cross to the community.
The Abbess, Etheldreda Mannock, was succeeded in
her office by Dame Mary Ursula Pigott — a name,
like that of Mannock, well-known in the English Benedictine *Fasti* of the last century, and to some persons,
perhaps, through the once well-known Catholic counsel,
Nathaniel Pigott, of Whitton, for whose family the
poet Pope, a near neighbour, entertained a high regard.
It was this Abbess who gave the cross to Mr. Weld.

During the office of Lady Abbess Pigott, the community were forced by the Revolution to leave Brussels,
and settled at Winchester, whence in 1857 they removed
to their present abbey at East Bergholt, near Colchester.

From the Welds the cross passed through Cardinal
Weld to his only daughter, Lady Clifford. It afterwards came into the possession of her son, the Hon.
and Right Reverend William Clifford, third Bishop
of Clifton, at whose decease it passed into the hands
of his nephew, the present Lord Clifford of Chudleigh,
to whose kindness I am indebted for these details and
the photographs of the cross reproduced in these pages.

ERRATUM.—P. 116, *note*, for line 7 and 8 *read :* "the letters of Russell and Pollard state that the abbot was executed on the Tor hill, the Roman editor of Sander uses only a general expression," &c.

INDEX.

13